THE CHALLENGES OF PRIVATIZATION

THE CHALLENGES OF PRIVATIZATION
An International Analysis

BERNARDO BORTOLOTTI
DOMENICO SINISCALCO

OXFORD
UNIVERSITY PRESS

OXFORD
UNIVERSITY PRESS

Great Clarendon Street, Oxford OX2 6DP

Oxford University Press is a department of the University of Oxford.
It furthers the University's objective of excellence in research, scholarship,
and education by publishing worldwide in

Oxford New York

Auckland Bangkok Buenos Aires Cape Town Chennai
Dar es Salaam Delhi Hong Kong Istanbul Karachi Kolkata
Kuala Lumpur Madrid Melbourne Mexico City Mumbai Nairobi
São Paulo Shanghai Taipei Tokyo Toronto

Oxford is a registered trade mark of Oxford University Press
in the UK and in certain other countries

Published in the United States
by Oxford University Press Inc., New York

© 2004 Bernardo Bortolotti and Domenico Siniscalco

The moral rights of the author have been asserted
Database right Oxford University Press (maker)

First published 2004

British Library Cataloguing in Publication Data
Data available

Library of Congress Cataloging in Publication Data
Data available
ISBN 0-19-924934-2

1 3 5 7 9 10 8 6 4 2

Typeset by Newgen Imaging Systems (P) Ltd., Chennai, India
Printed in Great Britain
on acid-free paper by
Biddles Ltd., King's Lynn, Norfolk

Preface

Between 1977 and 2001 more than 3,535 privatization operations were carried out in the world, bringing government revenues of over $1,127 billion. The phenomenon involved over 100 countries, and all sectors in which state-owned enterprises usually operate: agriculture and industry, finance, telecommunications, energy, and public utilities. Beyond aggregate figures, the process took different forms and yielded different outcomes in various countries.

This book presents a thorough empirical analysis that makes it possible to identify the main trends and patterns of privatization worldwide. However, it is not simply a collection of stylized facts. Rather, it aims at explaining why and how privatization takes place, trying to simplify the wider complexity of the process.

Our work has an underlying thesis. We try to prove that privatization has been a very varied process in different parts of the world, seldom decided upon autonomously, more often forced by external factors and carried out reluctantly in the absence of suitable legal, political, and economic institutions. As a result, in most cases, privatization has been incomplete and fraught with error. However, privatization is partly an irreversible process that may lead to institutional innovation and market development.

We argue that privatization outcomes can be explained by a unified framework suitable for understanding whether privatization is a trend or a cycle, for identifying the factors shaping the evolution of the process over time, and for considering why private ownership is likely to coexist with public control, at least in the near future.

B.B.
D.S.

Torino
23 April 2003

Acknowledgements

This book is based on a combination of real-world experiences and academic work. On the practical level, it owes much to direct experience on privatization sales conducted at the Department of the Treasury of the Italian Ministry of Economics and Finance. On the academic level, it has benefited from interaction with a number of academics involved in similar lines of research on privatization, corporate governance, and regulation.

Among these, special thanks go to Bill Megginson and Guido Tabellini. Bill shared his knowledge of privatization literature, helping us in the design of this editorial project. Guido's criticism and comments on earlier versions of the manuscript have been useful in improving the empirical tests and in developing new research hypotheses.

Comprehensive empirical analyses need large databases and assembling them is a long and tiring process. In this respect, we owe a debt of gratitude to Marcella Fantini, who helped us in the construction of most of the datasets used in the book and performed several econometric tests. Outstanding research assistance was provided during different stages of this project by Luca Sala, Claudia Panseri, Mara Grasseni, Cristian Galizzi, and Laura Poddi. We would especially like to thank Luca Farinola for his heroic efforts in chasing privatization data. We received excellent editorial assistance from Valentina Milella, who assembled the final manuscript, patiently prepared most figures and tables, and carefully checked references, remaining supportive and cheerful throughout.

We also wish to thank the co-authors of our academic work: Frank De Jong, Giovanna Nicodano, Paolo Pinotti, Carlo Scarpa, Ibolya Schindele, and Serena Vitalini for their insights and cooperation.

We received very useful comments on single chapters or on the entire book from Utpal Bhattacharya, William Baumol, Marco Becht, Bruno Biais, Eric Berglof, Carlo Carraro, Gabriella Chiesa, George Clark, Claude d'Aspremont, Gerrit de Marez Oyens, Mara Faccio, Francesco Giavazzi, Roger Gordon, Marzio Galeotti, Dirk Heremans, André Léger, Chong Ju Choi, David Newbery, Gérard Roland, Marco Pagano, David Parker, Enrico Perotti, Enrico Rettore, Alessandro Sembenelli, Mary Shirley, Andrei Shleifer, Jacques Thisse, and Luigi Zingales. Any remaining inaccuracies and errors can, obviously, only be blamed on us.

Finally, we would like to thank the referees, the OUP delegates, and particularly Andrew Schuller, for his support and patience.

This editorial project has been conceived and realized at the Fondazione Eni Enrico Mattei, in Milan. The Fondazione provided not only financial support, but also a stimulating research environment to develop, discuss, and disseminate our ideas.

Contents

List of Figures ix

List of Tables x

Introduction 1

1. The Economic Theory of Privatization 5
    1.1.   Introduction 5
    1.2.   Why privatize? Neutrality theorems 6
    1.3.   Ownership matters: the incomplete contracts approach 9
    1.4.   The political economics of privatization 12
    1.5.   The choice of the privatization method 16
    1.6.   Conclusions 19

2. Privatization Around the World 21
    2.1.   Introduction 21
    2.2.   The United Kingdom 23
    2.3.   Continental Europe 25
    2.4.   North America and the Caribbean 28
    2.5.   Latin America 30
    2.6.   Sub-Saharan Africa 32
    2.7.   The Middle East and North Africa 33
    2.8.   Asia 35
    2.9.   Oceania 37
    2.10. Central and Eastern European Countries and the former
          Soviet Union 38
    2.11. Conclusions 40

3. The Determinants of Privatization 41
    3.1.   Introduction 41
    3.2.   Privatization and economic development 42
    3.3.   Governments' budget constraints 45
    3.4.   The role of financial markets 46
    3.5.   Political majorities 48
    3.6.   Legal origins 49
    3.7.   Political institutions 51
    3.8.   Empirical results 54
    3.9.   Conclusions 58

4. How do Governments Privatize?   59
  4.1. Introduction   59
  4.2. Widening share ownership   60
  4.3. Credibility, commitment, and the structure of the offer   65
  4.4. Financial market development   68
  4.5. The political and economic consequences of privatization   70
  4.6. Conclusions   78

5. Private Ownership, Public Control   79
  5.1. Introduction   79
  5.2. Partial privatization   80
  5.3. The dynamics of state ownership in privatized firms   83
  5.4. Golden shares and special rights   88
  5.5. Measuring golden shares in strategic sectors   91
  5.6. Conclusions   97

6. Privatizing Monopolies   98
  6.1. Introduction   98
  6.2. Privatization, right and wrong: the case of Argentine utilities   103
  6.3. Privatizing electricity   105
  6.4. Vertical integration   108
  6.5. Market regulation   110
  6.6. Empirical results   113
  6.7. Conclusions   118

Conclusion   119

Appendix 1: Data and Methodology   121
  1. Privatization variables   121
  2. Political variables   121
  3. The control sample   130

Appendix 2: Importing Investor Protection   132
  1. Cross-listing procedures   132

Appendix 3: Golden Shares Around the World   135

References   145
Index   151

Figures

I.1 Privatization around the world (1977–2001)   2
2.1 Privatization around the world: ranking by transactions (1977–2001)   22
2.2 Privatization around the world: ranking by revenue (1977–2001)   22
2.3 Privatization around the world: revenue by sectors (1977–2001)   23
2.4 Privatization in the United Kingdom (1977–2001)   25
2.5 Privatization in Continental Europe (1977–2001)   27
2.6 Privatization in North America and the Caribbean (1977–2001)   29
2.7 Privatization in Latin America (1977–2001)   31
2.8 Privatization in sub-Saharan Africa (1977–2001)   33
2.9 Privatization in the Middle East and North Africa (1977–2001)   34
2.10 Privatization in Asia (1977–2001)   36
2.11 Privatization in Oceania (1977–2001)   37
2.12 Privatization in Eastern European Countries (CEECs) and the former Soviet Union (1977–2001)   39
4.1 Capitalization and trading value of privatized companies   73
5.1 Average residual stake and companies with golden shares at a country level   94
5.2 Average residual stake in companies with golden shares and its intensity at a country level   96
6.1 Distribution of revenue by sector around the world (1977–2001)   99
6.2 Distribution of revenue by sector in Western Europe (1977–2001)   99
6.3 Distribution of revenue by sector in Latin America (1977–2001)   100
6.4 Distribution of revenue by sector in Oceania (1977–2001)   100
6.5 Distribution of revenue by sector in the CEECs and the former Soviet Union (1977–2001)   101
6.6 Distribution of revenue by sector in Mena (1977–2001)   101
6.7 Distribution of revenue by sector in Asia (1977–2001)   102
6.8 Distribution of revenue by sector in sub-Saharan Africa (1977–2001)   102
6.9 Distribution of revenue by sector in North America and the Caribbean (1977–2001)   103
6.10 Entel prices (1988–1992)   104

Tables

2.1 Average percentage of privatized stock by sector and by
    privatization method (1977–2001)   26
3.1 Privatization across countries   43
3.2 Privatization revenue/GDP (around the world, 1977–1999: Tobit)   55
3.3 Privatization revenue/GDP (OECD countries, 1977–1999: Tobit)   57
4.1 Privatization on public equity markets   62
4.2 Probability of an international share issue privatization (ISIP)
    and the percentage of shares sold abroad   63
4.3 The impact of privatization on financial markets   72
5.1 Explaining partial sales   82
5.2 Ultimate ownership in privatized companies   85
5.3 Ultimate ownership (UO) in privatized vs. matching (private)
    firms   87
5.4 Intensity of the golden shares (as of 2002)   92
5.5 Residual average stake and golden shares   95
6.1 Privatization in electricity generation (1977–1997)   106
6.2 Privatization in the electricity sector, regulation, and vertical
    integration   114
6.3 Privatization sales in electricity generation (Tobit)   115
6.4 Privatization revenue in electricity generation (Tobit)   115
6.5 The percentage of capital sold in electricity generation (OLS)   117
A1.1 Privatization variables   122
A1.2 Economic and financial variables   124
A1.3 Political variables   126
A1.4 Institutional variables   128
A1.5 Industrial sectors   130
A1.6 Control sample   131
A3.1 Golden shares around the world   139

Introduction

Privatization, that is, the transfer of ownership rights from the public to the private sector, is one of the main events of the economic and financial history of the post-war period.

The milestones of privatization history can be sketched briefly as follows. One of the first privatizations in modern times was undertaken by the Adenauer government in the Federal Republic of Germany. In 1961, the German government launched a policy of denationalization of the economy and sold a majority stake in Volkswagen through a public offering, mainly earmarked for small investors. This was followed by the sale of Veba shares in 1965. Both offers were well received initially but, at the first stock market slump, the government was forced to bail out investors, and reversed the stated policy. Other failed attempts occurred in Chile and Ireland at the beginning of the 1970s.

The story picks up in 1979 in the United Kingdom under Mrs Margaret Thatcher's Conservative government, which, indeed, coined the term 'privatization' in place of the less attractive 'denationalization'.[1] Interestingly, privatization had not been one of the prominent themes of the electoral campaign that brought the Conservatives to victory. Nevertheless, the Thatcher government's policy of SOEs (state-owned enterprises) assets disposal left a lasting mark on the economic history of the twentieth century.

At the beginning, the programme met with the scepticism of economists, the media, and commentators in general, so much so that the opposition Labour Party promised to return to public ownership the assets privatized if it returned to power. Within a few years, thanks to the success of many privatizations, the Conservatives obtained a wide political support which allowed them to accomplish the process. At the end of the fourth Conservative legislature in 1997, virtually all SOEs were sold out, with their value accounting for a marginal share of GDP (Vickers and Yarrow 1988; World Bank 1995).

During the 1990s the privatization policy became a fundamental element of global economic orthodoxy, spreading out in developed, emerging, and less developed countries.

The rationale for a privatization policy can be found in recent economic literature but it can be also be traced back to Adam Smith (1776: 771). Smith observed that 'characters do not exist who are more distant than the sovereign and the entrepreneur', in that people are more generous with the resources of

---

[1] The word 'privatization' does not appear in dictionaries until the middle of the 1980s.

others than their own, and that public administration could lead to an inefficient use of assets because public employees do not have a direct interest in the economic performance of their own actions.

According to Smith (1776: 785), the sale of public property (which at the time was land) also had another effect: revenue can be allocated to reduce public debt; and lower interest charges alleviate public finances in greater measure than the ownership of the land. With privatization therefore, efficiency is increased. Stated in the terms of modern contract theory, this occurs because ownership rights are not neutral but affect the profitability of companies.

As often happens, simple intuitions have the ring of truth. After twenty years of modern experience, Adam Smith's intuition has been amply confirmed. Thanks to the transfer of ownership rights, privatized companies have greatly improved their efficiency. And the countries that have privatized have reduced their public debts and deficits.

The big privatization cycle of the 1990s is now over. After the peak in 1999, global revenues have fallen sharply at an average annual rate of 46 per cent, reaching a value of $44 billion in 2001, and the data for 2002 and 2003 seem to confirm this negative trend (see Figure I.1). Similar figures date back to the late 1980s, when Mrs Thatcher's privatization reached its climax, but the rest of the world was still standing on the sidelines.

Privatization now seems exhausted, especially in Europe, the continent most involved in the phenomenon. Why is this so? Are Adam Smith's lessons about private property no longer valid, or is the process shrinking simply because governments do not have any more property to sell or because sales in times of bad economic outlook are more difficult?

This book is a comprehensive study of the privatization cycle of the 1990s, of its determinants, methods, and economic and financial consequences. The analyses that we present shed some light on the past process, but are also useful for understanding the actual stalemate, and the challenges that we will face in the future.

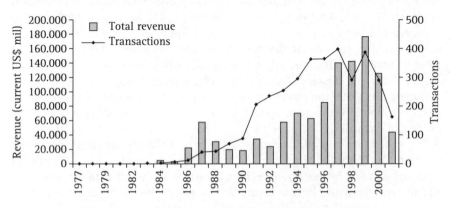

Figure I.1. *Privatization around the world (1977–2001)*

Source: Elaboration on *Privatisation International*, and *Securities Data Corporation*.

Extant empirical research has already led to some important conclusions on these themes. These are summarized by Megginson and Netter's (2001) influential survey:

(i) privatization has halved the weight of SOEs within the GDP of industrialized countries but has progressed with greater difficulty in less developed countries;

(ii) the efficiency of privatized companies in terms of productivity and growth has, on average, increased more than that of companies left in public hands; profitability has also increased but the evidence about the effects of privatization and lay-offs is quite mixed;

(iii) when privatization occurs in public equity markets, underpricing (a discount on the companies' effective value) is often necessary to favour the sale; therefore investors who purchase shares at the Initial Public Offer (IPO) earn significantly positive market-adjusted returns;

(iv) a large privatization programme based on issues on public equity markets is a spur to modernizing a nation's corporate governance system.

These conclusions are now generally accepted. But why does the extent of privatization vary so greatly across countries? How do governments trade off their conflicting objectives in the designing of the sales? Furthermore, does privatization really entail a dramatic change in governance structure or do governments still hang on to control with direct or indirect means? Finally, how do regulation and institutional changes affects privatization outcomes?

This book tries to provide some answers to these important questions. First, it offers a selective survey of the theoretical models from which empirical predictions can be drawn (Chapter 1). Then it puts research hypotheses to the test, carrying out statistical analyses on a great number of operations, in a great number of countries, and over a period of more than twenty years. In summary, the results of our investigation are as follows:

(i) The big privatization cycle starting in the 1980s and ending at the turn of the century is common to all economic areas and to almost all sectors; however, the timing, methods, and results of privatization have varied greatly in different areas of the world (Chapter 2).

(ii) Privatization is determined by political preferences and shaped by economic and institutional constraints. Indeed, privatization is associated with right-wing majorities in office, driven by poor fiscal conditions and booming stock markets, and limited by proportional electoral rules granting power to veto players (Chapter 3).

(iii) Governments tend to privatize to widen share ownership, to gain credibility over time, and to develop domestic stock markets. Overall, suitably chosen privatization methods allow them to target these objectives (Chapter 4).

(iv) The privatization process has been partial and incomplete. The government still controls directly or indirectly, through *golden shares*, large parts of the national economy. This reluctance to sell can be traced back partly to weak legal protection of investors and to governments' willingness to maintain political control in strategic sectors (Chapter 5).

(v) In the privatization of monopolies, finally, the pre-existence of a well defined regulatory structure favours divestiture, reducing uncertainty and contributing to the enhancement of the company's value (Chapter 6).

Beyond single results, the overall message of the book is straightforward. The sale of SOEs' assets took place in all parts of the world, sometimes spontaneously, more often under the pressure of economic and financial constraints. Several goals have been met, but despite proclamations and programmes only a small minority of countries have carried out a genuine privatization process— completely transferring ownership and control of SOEs to the private sector. As we shall see, the state is still an influential shareholder in several privatized companies. The current stalemate cannot therefore be ascribed to the fact that there is no state-ownership left to privatize.

At root there is undoubtedly a lack of political will; in other words, governments are unwilling to relinquish the political power associated with control of SOEs. But lack of political will can be traced partly to structural factors that would make an orderly privatization difficult. These include the absence of developed capital markets and suitable institutions.

This framework of difficulties, however, is neither static nor irremediable. In fact, privatization has sometimes contributed to the removal of such barriers and gradually created the premises for its own success. This has happened when sales have been accompanied by a process of learning and structural reform, creating irreversibility. In this matter, privatization is a truly cumulative process rather than a list of sales. We believe this to be the right approach to privatization, especially in emerging countries and in transition economies. The dogmatic application of privatization policy has resulted in some recent failures in Asia, Russia, and Latin America. However, the error stemmed not from the decision to privatize but rather from the idea that privatization is a simple process, one in which developed markets and legal institutions spontaneously come into being after the sale. In fact, they do not. Privatization brings about widespread benefits only if sales are accompanied by intentional structural reform.

Our view contrasts with the 'big bang' approach light-heartedly set forth by international economic institutions in recent years, and contributes to a more knowing and problematic vision of privatization and liberalization; a process needed to promote development and welfare, particularly in the poorer regions of the world.

According to the available research there are a huge number of companies to be privatized. China and India have probably the largest revenue potential, together with residual state holding in European companies (*Privatization International Yearbook* 2000). The lessons of history have, therefore, plenty of room for application.

1

The Economic Theory of Privatization

1.1. INTRODUCTION

The economists' debate about the proper scope of government in the economy is as old as the economics discipline. Therefore we leave to historians of the economic school the daunting task of tracing back the evolution of this debate.[1] The purpose of this chapter is less ambitious, as it aims to provide a concise survey of the main results in the economic theory of privatization.

This field of research started developing in the 1980s and burgeoned during the 1990s, parallelling the spreading out of the privatization process around the world and with the advance of the contract, political economy, and auction theories.

Curiously, the United Kingdom embarked on the first large-scale privatization programme in the late 1970s largely on faith, as the main privatization theories were not yet developed. As Vickers and Yarrow (1988) note, the UK programme was triggered mainly by dissatisfaction with the performance of the SOE sector and by the need to square public finances. It was certainly not worked out as the Cartesian application of sophisticated theories, but by adopting a practical approach based on the intuitions of some great economists of the past, such as Hayek.[2] However, the UK path-breaking experience was important not only for practical reasons, but also because it provided economists with a laboratory for empirical analyses, allowing the testing of hypotheses and the development of new theories.

This chapter is organized as follows: it starts by introducing several irrelevance results showing that private or public ownership may not matter for the behaviour of firms. These neutrality results are useful benchmarks which hold under strong assumptions, the main one being a government's complete contracting ability. When incomplete contracts are introduced, ownership and governance structure are shown to matter, as they dramatically alter incentives with important consequences for company performance. The incomplete contract approach has strong normative implications which allow for the identification of the costs and benefits of privatization. However, this approach

---

[1] A concise but effective historical survey on economic thinking about government ownership is provided by Shleifer (1998).

[2] For an account of Hayek (1994) on privatization policy see Yergin and Stanislaw (1998).

typically assumes that a government's objectives are exogenously given. The political economy approach takes a further step by modelling explicitly the political process underlying privatization policy. This approach argues that privatization has important distributive consequences and that the preferences of the median voter are the key to explaining the feasibility and irreversibility of privatization. Finally, the chapter analyses the optimal privatization method in relation to the various economic and political objectives, drawing extensively from the recent achievements in auctions theory and finance.

Obviously, this survey is far from being complete. The reader may refer to Sheshinski and Lòpez Calva (2000) and to Shirley and Walsh (2000) for a more comprehensive account of the literature. However, it reflects the authors' views about which are the most influential contributions, and provides the theoretical backing for the empirical analyses that will be performed in the following chapters.

1.2. WHY PRIVATIZE? NEUTRALITY THEOREMS

To address correctly the theoretical analysis of privatization, one should beg the following question: what is the proper role of the state in the production of goods and services in the economy?

A useful starting point can be represented by the two fundamental theorems of welfare economics: (a) the competitive equilibrium is Pareto-efficient; (b) any Pareto-efficient allocation can be supported by a competitive equilibrium. For these two theorems to be true, several strong assumptions must hold. First, markets must be perfectly competitive; second, there must not be any deviation from private and social costs or benefits (externalities); third, no public good has to be consumed and produced; fourth, agents must be perfectly informed. Finally, lump-sum transfers must be feasible. Under these assumptions, there is no role for the state in production. Basically, it just has to enforce property rights over the assets, and organize a more equitable redistribution of resources thorough non-distortionary fiscal policy, giving free rein to market forces and private ownership.

Clearly, the assumptions underlying the welfare theorems are too restrictive. When these are relaxed, several market failures emerge so that an efficient allocation of resources is no longer guaranteed by the operating of markets forces alone. And it is easy to show that there is scope for an active role for government in the economic system.

However, even if efficiency dictates that the government has to be engaged in the *provision* of goods and services, it is not clear whether the government should be directly involved in the *production*, nor the delegation of private firms to produce these goods in its place. In that respect, the economic literature has set forth several neutrality theorems, establishing the conditions under which the private or public ownership of productive assets is irrelevant for the final allocation of resources. Clearly, these models do not imply that ownership is actually neutral, but have to be interpreted as useful benchmarks for developing richer models where privatization is *not* neutral.

Sappington and Stiglitz (1987) were the first to establish an irrelevance result, known as the 'fundamental privatization theorem':

Suppose that the government pursues the following objectives: (i) economic efficiency; (ii) equity; (iii) rent extraction. Then the government can design an auction scheme so that it can meet 'perfectly' these objectives, and public production cannot improve upon private production.

The argument runs as follows. The government has a 'social' valuation of the level of output, which embodies equity considerations such as the consumption levels of the good among different classes of citizens. Production has to be carried out by two (or more) risk-neutral firms, who have symmetric beliefs about the least-cost production technology. The government auctions off the right to produce the output and to receive a payment which equals the social evaluation. The most efficient firm will win the contract with the highest bid, and will set the production level most preferred by the government. The mechanism implements an efficient allocation, and if the auction is sufficiently competitive, it will allow a complete rent extraction through the price chosen *ex ante*.

Shapiro and Willig (1990) obtain a similar result in a setting where a social planner, or framer, evaluates the nationalization/privatization decision by considering the informational difference between state-owned and private (publicly regulated) firms. Three pieces of information are crucial in this context: (i) the information about the external social benefits of the enterprise's activity; (ii) the information about the divergence between the public interest and the interest (private agenda) of the regulator; and (iii) the information about the profitability of the firm.

Under the state's ownership, the company is managed by a public official (a minister). As manager, the minister knows about the profitability of the SOE, and by virtue of his position, he also knows about the externalities generated by the operations of the company. On the basis of this information, he has to decide whether to authorize the investment in the company, and the level of output. The minister maximizes an objective function which is made up of two components: social welfare, and private benefits of control. The second term is weighted by a parameter measuring how easily the minister can extract these benefits, which can be interpreted as a proxy for the effectiveness of the political system: indeed, a well-functioning political system limits the opportunity for public officials to pursue private interests.

Under private regulated ownership, the company is managed by a professional manager, who observes the profitability of the firm, overseen also by a regulator, who observes the externality variable and the private agenda variable. The regulator sets an incentive scheme such that if the firm chooses a given output level, the company receives a given transfer from the public sector. The regulatory contract must be such as to ensure non-negative profits to the firm. In this context, the firm maximizes the profits in response to the regulatory scheme, and the regulator has the same objective function as the minister under state ownership. Finally, the framer maximizes the total surplus net of the cost of raising public funds.

The main difference between public and private ownership is the location of the information about cost and demand conditions. Under private ownership, the manager is the informed party, while under the state's ownership the information resides with the minister. Privatization therefore erects an informational barrier between the state and the firm, which comes with costs and benefits. On the one hand, the informational barrier creates an agency problem so that it is more difficult for the public official to motivate the firm to pursue social objectives. But on the other hand, it reduces the discretion of the public official who could also pursue a private agenda in the management of the firm.

There are cases in which the performance of public and private firms is equivalent, the obvious one being the full information case, when the regulator can implement a set of taxes and subsidies contingent upon each realization of the random variables of the model, inducing the firm to serve precisely the interests of the regulator. But this equivalence can also be proved in more interesting cases with private information.

Assume that the private information about the firm's profitability is known only *after* the investment is made. Then, the regulator can implement a mechanism forcing the firm to internalize the objectives of the regulator. Alternatively, assume that private information is privately known by the firm before the investment is made, but that there is no cost of raising public funds. In that case, the transfer of any amount can be implemented, and the regulated private firm chooses the same activity level chosen by the public firms. Clearly, the amount of funds transferred is greater, but since the drain does not come with costs, the framer is indifferent between the two forms of organizations.

Shleifer and Vishny's (1994) starting point is that politicians control SOEs in order to achieve political objectives, such as excess employment and high wages. The politician derives benefits from this inefficient allocation of resources, as they create political support for the incumbent government. When the company is privatized, the politician bargains with the manager/owner of the firm, who aims instead at maximizing profits. Clearly, the manager and the politician have conflicting objectives, as the firm maximizes profits when the manager does not hire any extra employees. In order to persuade the manager, the politician can subsidize the firm, making a transfer from the Treasury. However, this transfer is costly for the politician, as taxes have to be raised to finance the subsidy.

The model also allows for a complete separation of ownership rights and control rights. Instead of a clear-cut dichotomy between state-owned and private firms, the model encompasses four possible categories: (i) a typical SOE, when the Treasury owns most of the equity, and politician has control rights; (ii) a regulated firm, when the private sector owns most of the equity, but the politician has control rights and can interfere in the operating activity of the firm; (iii) a 'corporatized' firm, when the government has cash flow rights, but relinquishes control to the management; (iv) a purely private firm, when the manager/owner has ownership and control rights.

Before analysing the equilibrium of the bargaining game, the authors identify the two allocations when the politician and the manager control the SOE, respectively. These allocations will be the disagreement points of the bargaining game. Under politician control, the politician has power over the manager, and keeps the firm down to zero profits, and uses the firm's cash flow to hire extra labour up to the point where the marginal benefits of the excess employment equals the marginal cost of raising public funds. On the contrary, under manager control, the manager has power over the politician, and the firm produces at the efficient level (with zero excess labour) but does not receive any transfer from the Treasury.

Efficiency—from the point of view of the manager and politician, not society— dictates that the manager and the politician raise extra employment to the point where the marginal political benefits equal the marginal cost, i.e. the wage. At the efficient point, excess labour is lower than under politician control, and the subsidy from the Treasury is higher than under managerial control.

The most interesting finding of Shleifer and Vishny's analysis is again a neutrality result, which is a straightforward application of the Coase theorem to privatization. When side payments are allowed, or more bluntly, when the manager and politician can freely bribe each other, then the manager and the politician reach the (jointly) efficient solution independently of the initial allocation of ownership and control rights. With full corruption, neither privatization nor corporatization matters for the final allocation of resources. In highly corrupted environments, the manager and the politician bargain to internalize fully the inefficiencies, and the same level of extra employment is reached regardless of whom has ownership and control rights over the firm. However, the allocation of control rights affects bribes.

1.3. OWNERSHIP MATTERS: THE INCOMPLETE CONTRACTS APPROACH

The empirical validity of these neutrality theorems is questionable as striking differences are observed in the operational performance of private firms as compared to SOEs. On closer inspection, the irrelevance results hinge upon a crucial assumption, i.e. that complete contingent long-term contracts can be written and enforced. In reality, surplus from economic activity usually emerges from relationship specific investments, which cannot be contracted upon by involved parties. A typical example is the amount of effort deployed by a manager to restructure a firm and to reorganize production. Effort on-the-job is usually non-verifiable and sunk, so that its payoff is subject to expropriation. As a consequence, long-term specific investments tend to be sub-optimal. When only incomplete contracts are feasible, ownership affects dramatically the performance and efficiency of firms (Williamson 1985; Grossman and Hart 1986).

Privatization represents an interesting application of this analytical approach. Indeed, incomplete contracts explain why privatization *does* matter, i.e. why state-owned firms may behave differently from privatized firms.

Schmidt (1996) considers a monopolistic firm producing a public good. In the initial period, the government has to decide whether to privatize the firm by selling it to an owner-manager or whether to keep it publicly owned and hire a professional manager. As in Shapiro and Willig (1990), information about costs is private information of the owner of the firm, so that privatization entails a reallocation of private information.

In a subsequent period, the manager has to choose the effort level and then the state of the world is realized. The level of effort chosen affects the probability of the state of the world so that if the managers exert a high level of effort, productive efficiency will be enhanced and costs will be lower for any level of output. In the final period, the government decides the transfer scheme and payoffs are realized.

When the firm is state owned, the government observes directly the realized parameter of the cost structure and therefore implements the first-best allocation, by choosing the *ex post* efficient production level. However, given that contingent contracts are not feasible, the manager's wage will be fixed and independent from the level of output. As compensation is fixed, the manager has no incentive to exert any effort. Anticipating this, the government will offer the manager only his reservation wage.

On the contrary, when the firm is privatized, the government does not know the exact cost function of the firm. In order to induce the private owner to produce an efficient level of output, the government must give him an incentive in the form of an informational rent. If transfers are costly, it will not be possible to implement the optimal allocation, and the private owner will set an inefficient low production level. However, given that the probability of obtaining the rent is an increase in effort, the manager under privatization has more incentives to invest.

The main conclusion is the following. When the monopolistic firm produces a good yielding a social benefit, privatization involves a trade-off between allocative and productive efficiency. Equilibrium production levels are not socially optimal, but the better managerial incentives allow for saving costs. The net welfare effect of privatization should therefore be unambiguously positive when the social benefit from production is small. On the contrary, public ownership should be the most appropriate governance structure in vital industries with large social externalities.

The normative implications of this model are important as a case for privatization can also be made when the government is a fully benevolent dictator maximizing social welfare. Even if it were possible to correct all the potential deficiencies of the political system (such as rent-seeking, corruption, and politicians pursuing a private agenda, etc.), privatization would still be superior to state ownership.

Shapiro and Willig (1990) draw a similar conclusion in a context where the regulator may pursue a different agenda from the framer. Again, ownership is no more neutral when information about profitability is known before the investment decision is made, and where there is a dead weight loss of raising public funds. The equilibrium behaviour of the minister of the public firm is virtually unconstrained, and he will simply set the activity levels of the SOE to maximize his utility. Under private ownership, the regulator has instead to solve a more complex model, which involves the design of a regulatory incentive scheme for the firm ensuring non-negative profits. As typically happens in the models of optimal regulation under asymmetric information, the firm enjoys an informational rent, which is directly proportional to the activity chosen, and costly for the state, given the burden of raising public funds.

We now come to the basic trade-off. If the public official's objectives coincide with those of the framer, then private ownership reduces performance, as the firm extracts a positive rent. But if the public official pursues a private agenda, then a reduced discretion may improve welfare. Indeed, politicians can more easily distort the operating activity of the company to favour their interests if it is state owned and fully controlled by the minister. Under regulated private ownership, the firm earns a positive rent, but it is less subject to the influence of the regulator. Therefore private (regulated) firms perform better in poorly functioning political systems, and private information concerning profitability is less significant.

In a similar vein, Laffont and Tirole (1991) consider the case of a firm producing a public good. In order to ensure production, the firm's manager has to invest in assets which can be redeployed to serve social goals. For example, the government may reduce the return of the investment on some facilities (e.g. networks) by granting *ex post* access to the general population. This decision would be socially optimal, but it would also be an expropriation of the firm's investment. Hence the manager will be reluctant to invest in a state-owned firm, as he rationally foresees that the government will interfere. Incentives to invest in privatized firms are higher because shareholders' incentives are aligned with the manager's, as both are interested in profit maximization. However, private ownership comes with costs. Now the manager has to serve two masters with conflicting objectives: the government, pursuing allocative efficiency, and the shareholders seeking profit maximization. Both have incomplete information about the firm's costs and have to offer incentive schemes. The multi-principal structure of the game concedes a large informational rent to the manager, leading to a larger distortion of production than if the manager contracted only with the government. The trade-off identified in this model is similar to that described by Schmidt (1996). However, the model fails to identify precise conditions under which privatization is superior to nationalization.

Finally, Hart, Shleifer, and Vishny (1997) de-emphasize informational problems presenting a model of contracting out where the provider of the service can invest his time either to improve the quality of the service or to reduce its costs. The key assumption is that any investment to curb costs has a negative effect on quality. As usual, investments are not contractible *ex ante*. When the provider of the service is a public employee, he needs government approval to implement any innovation. The employee will obtain only a fraction of the return on the investment as the government enjoys residual rights. When the provider is a private contractor, he will have stronger incentives both to increase quality and to save costs. The problem of contracting out is that incentives to cut costs are very strong and the private firm does not fully internalize the adverse consequences on quality of the cost reduction. On the contrary, public ownership removes the excessive incentives to cost reduction replacing them with weak incentives to innovate. Shleifer (1998) lists the following conditions under which public ownership should be superior: when (i) costs reductions are associated with a significant non-contractible deterioration in quality; (ii) innovation is relatively unimportant; (iii) competition is weak and consumer choice ineffective; (iv) reputational mechanisms are not operational. Indeed, the stringency of these conditions suggests a narrow scope for government ownership of productive assets.

1.4. THE POLITICAL ECONOMICS OF PRIVATIZATION

The incomplete contract approach has a strong normative content and provides a useful framework for evaluating the costs and benefits of privatization. Yet government preferences are exogenously given. In some models, the government is a benevolent agent maximizing social welfare, in others it has a political agenda and seeks to maintain political support.

Some recent contributions have tried to model more deeply the political incentives and constraints shaping divestiture. The maintained assumption of this field of research is that privatization has strong distributional consequences so that voters' preferences are the key in understanding how this policy is implemented. Indeed, privatization policy tends to create unemployment if inefficient SOEs are heavily restructured by the new owners. Excess unemployment can create a backlash against privatization and induce politicians to policy reversals and re-nationalizations.

These observations are the starting point of Roland and Verdier (1994). In their model, at the initial stage all firms in the economy are offered to the private investors (i.e. privatized). Then investors have to decide to enter and restructure the firms, incurring a fixed sunk cost. At a second stage, government observes the level of effective privatization achieved and decides to re-nationalize if that level is lower than expected. Finally production takes place and unemployment occurs.

The government maximizes the expected utility of the average citizen. In this context, privatization involves the following trade-off. A higher number of privatizations increases the probability of unemployment, but at the same time it increases the income of the employed as redundant workers are no longer subsidized with taxation. The optimum number of privatizations will obviously equalize the marginal costs and benefits of privatization. Investors decide whether to enter or not, taking into account the risk of re-nationalization and the sunk entry cost. According to the size of these costs, there is a unique equilibrium with full, partial privatization, or re-nationalization.

Equilibria are no longer unique when positive externalities to the size of the private sector are assumed. Indeed, a larger private economy generates important spillovers and complementarities, as more inputs of higher quality can be available. Furthermore, non-rival inputs such as knowledge, research, and development, or a diffuse business community generate economies of scale.

When positive externalities are assumed, privatization does not necessarily increase the probability of unemployment, which could instead decrease if the number of privatizations is sufficiently large. The most important implication of this assumption is the existence of a *critical mass* of privatizations generating multiple equilibria. Above the threshold, the economy experiences a virtuous circle of increased efficiency and job creation, so that privatization becomes irreversible. Investment below this critical mass will instead create the risk of policy reversal up to the point where the marginal benefit of privatization equals the cost.

Is it possible to help the investor to solve this coordination problem and reach the best outcome? The authors analyse the effect of give-away privatization (i.e. the free distribution of shares and dividends) showing that under plausible circumstances this policy may counterbalance the negative effect of privatization on unemployment, making full privatization the only possible equilibrium.

The incentives to policy reversals and re-nationalization are also studied by Schmidt (2000). The main difference with respect to Roland and Verdier's (1994) analysis are twofold: first, unemployment is not an unavoidable consequence of restructuring, but it may or may not occur depending on how successful restructuring has been; second, the government can opt for different privatization strategies such as diversified or insider mass privatization. The paper has been written with a focus on transition economies. However, we think that its implications are far more general, and may also apply to more advanced economies. Indeed, a programme of public offerings with substantial shares earmarked to retail investors could be assimilated to a diversified mass privatization, whereas a preferential allocation of shares to SOEs employees displays similar features to an insider mass privatization.

The timing of the game is the following. At the initial stage, the government decides the fraction of shares to be sold to the strategic investor in each firm, and how to distribute the residual stake (i.e. either to the population at large, or to the insiders of the firm). At the second stage, strategic investors take over the firms, and decide the level of effort to deploy in restructuring. Effort affects the probability of successful restructuring. After restructuring, elections take place, and a policy shift is possible. Indeed, without commitment, the incumbent government cannot bind future governments not to expropriate private investors in order to subsidize unsuccessful firms. Expropriation can be interpreted as an unexpected review of the regulation, or outright re-nationalization, and takes the form of a 'tax' on the profits of successful firms. The expropriation rate chosen by the newly elected government will reflect the preferences of the median voter. At the final stage, uncertainty about restructuring efforts resolves, and payoffs are realized.

When the government chooses diversified mass privatization, it is shown that if workers are risk averse, an increase in the number of shares allocated to the population at large reduces the equilibrium expropriation rate. The intuition is straightforward. If the worker owns shares, then first, expropriation is more costly for him; second, he is richer. As a consequence, he has lower incentives to insure himself against bad states through expropriation. Incentives to 'buy' this insurance device are obviously higher under insider privatization, as workers now own a less diversified portfolio.

An important policy issue is whether the government should allow the immediate trading of the shares or whether it should create incentives to keep them. If the government's objective is to limit expropriation and create political support to privatization, the model shows that the first option is preferable. Indeed, if the median voter does not own shares any longer, he will prefer to expropriate as much as possible.

Clearly, diversified mass privatization allows for the reduction of the risks of expropriation and satisfies *ex post* political constraints. However, it has a cost in terms of productive efficiency as the incentives to restructure will be reduced as long as the stake owned by core investors is diluted. However, there can be an interior solution for the percentage of shares sold to the strategic investor where the level of expropriation is low, and all firms restructure, making positive profits. Giving away a fraction of shares therefore allows the government to maximize privatization revenues.

Biais and Perotti (2002) provide the first explicit assessment of the political aspects of privatization in a partisan model *à la* Aghion and Bolton (1990), showing how policy outcomes can create support for a given political platform and allow incumbent governments to achieve re-election. There are three socio-economic classes and two political parties: the right wing, maximizing the utility of the rich, and the left wing, maximizing the utility of the poor. Neither party has the majority, and both need the votes of the middle class to be elected. Parties cannot commit to a policy which will not be *ex post* optimal for their constituency. If the SOE is privatized, shares are partly sold to the manager, and partly to the different socio-economic classes. As usual, the manager can exert effort. If this is the case, the company is profitable. As in previous models, the government may interfere *ex post* by re-nationalizing the firm and allocating value to its most preferred constituency. Obviously, this policy has adverse consequences on the manager's incentives.

The sequence of the events is as follows. In the initial period, the incumbent party chooses the fiscal policy (i.e. a tax rate and a level of expenditures) and sets a privatization scheme. Then, elections take place. In the second period, the government again implements the preferred fiscal policy and decides whether or not to expropriate the shareholders by re-nationalizing the firm. Then the manager decides whether to exert effort. Finally, profits are realized and distributed or, in the case of re-nationalization, the government can target transfers from the SOE to its preferred constituency.

Suppose that at the initial period in which privatization takes place the right wing is in power. What will the economic policy of the right wing be in the second period? Recall that its objective is simply to maximize the utility of the rich. As to fiscal policy, the right wing will not be involved in any redistribution to the poor and will set the minimum level of taxation. As to re-nationalization, the right wing will not expropriate the privatized firm if the stake of the wealthy class is large enough. Importantly, it can be shown that the size of the critical stake owned by the rich is decreasing in income inequality. Indeed, if the middle class is poor, the rich will bear a larger part of the burden of taxation to cover targeted redistribution, so that re-nationalization becomes less attractive.

Suppose instead that the left wing is in power. The left wing government is keen to maximize resources available for redistribution. Therefore it will fully tax income, and certainly nationalize the firm. This policy is not politically costly, given that the poor do not hold any share. Given that re-nationalization will occur with certainty, the manager will not exert any effort, and the profit of the firm will be zero. The left will use the re-nationalized firm to target transfer to its most preferred class, and the losses of the SOEs will be covered by the budget.

The comparison of the payoffs of the median voter in the two alternative political scenarios allows the establishment of conditions under which the right wing wins the elections. This occurs when a substantial amount of shares are allocated to the middle class. This policy makes it averse to the redistribution policy of the left, so that privatization becomes irreversible as in Roland and Verdier (1994).

It is important to note that the higher the social inequality in the economy (i.e. the lower the median voter's income) the more difficult it is to entice the middle class to support the market oriented policies of the right wing. In this context, underpricing may be a privatization strategy aiming at buying out political consensus from the middle class. When inequality is extreme, under plausible conditions it can take the form of give-away privatization where assets are transferred for free. In this case, privatization at a higher price would not be feasible, as at this price the quantity of shares subscribed by the median voter would not be sufficient to avoid the election of the left wing.

This model allows for the rationalization of the stated objective of the development of popular capitalism which is often found in several privatization programmes by right wing governments. However, this theoretical prediction would be at odds with the stylized fact that the left wing is also involved in divestiture. Biais and Perotti (2002) consider this case in analysing privatization strategies of the left. Interestingly, they show that the left may also privatize with re-election concerns. However, the left does not underprice shares, but on the contrary tries to maximize privatization revenues available for redistribution. For this policy to succeed, the left must credibly commit not to re-nationalize the firm. Thus a substantial amount of shares has to be allocated to the poor.

1.5. THE CHOICE OF THE PRIVATIZATION METHOD

The normative analysis contained in the previous sections has allowed us to conclude that privatization, under well-specified conditions, may generate substantial welfare improvements. But once the privatization decision is taken, which is the optimal method for privatizing SOEs?

Clearly, there is no obvious answer to this question. In the real world, there is no one ideal method as every technique has its pros and cons. A useful approach is to set out the main privatization objectives, and then try to identify the most suitable methods for achieving them.

The previous section has clarified that privatization can be strategically designed to create irreversibility and achieve political goals such as re-election. In this part, we will look at more usual rationales such as efficiency, revenues, credibility, and financial market development which can be consistently pursued via privatization policy.

Revenues and Efficiency

Suppose that a government seeks to achieve an efficient allocation of ownership rights (i.e. it would like to allocate the privatized assets to those who value them most). Under a well-specified set of assumptions, the correct privatization method is simply to auction off the company and sell it to the highest bidder. Vickrey (1961) has proved that this proposition holds when bidders are risk neutral, *ex ante* all identical, and have independent private values (IPV). The last assumption is particularly important and says that each bidder has a personal valuation of the assets on sale which is not correlated with that of the other bidders. Importantly, it can be shown that the efficient outcome can be achieved through any auction format, and that revenues are equivalent across formats.

However, implementing this simple auction is not the best policy in order to maximize revenues. Indeed, posting a reserve price would allow the government to extract more surplus from the bidder. In simple IPV auctions, the price paid equals the second highest bid. Therefore government revenue may be higher if the valuation of the second highest is lower than the reserve price. However, the introduction of the reserve price has a cost as there is a chance that the company will not be sold. This happens when the highest bid is lower than the reserve price. Auctions with reserve prices introduce a source of inefficiency: the company is not sold even if the buyer has a higher valuation than the seller. Thus it may be difficult for divesting governments to commit credibly to an *ex post* inefficient selling mechanism, even if it could yield higher proceeds.

Relaxing each of the strong assumptions underlying the revenue equivalence theorem complicates matters considerably. However, by reviewing the main results of the recent economic theory of auctions applied in the privatization context, Schmidt and Schnitzer (1997) conclude that, under a wide variety of circumstance the so-called English (i.e. ascending bid first-price) auction tends to be efficient and allows for the maximization of revenue, especially when a government opts for a full disclosure policy. Interestingly, revealing all the available information allows the bidders to evaluate more precisely the future prospects of the company. This in turn improves the efficiency of the final allocation, and drives up the expected revenue as investors will bid more aggressively.

Cornelli and Li (1997) analyse privatization schemes in the context of optimal auction design. When large shareholders differ in terms of the public value of the firm under their control and the private benefits they would extract from the company, the government faces a trade-off between revenue and efficiency. The highest bidder may not be the most efficient shareholder, as his high bid may reflect his high private benefits of control. Privatization schemes may be designed by the government to screen among investors with different plans, choosing the most efficient investor by use of the number of shares sold. It is shown that the government maximizes his pay-off by making the allocation of shares contingent upon the bids, instead of committing to sell a fixed number of shares. This privatization mechanism screens the most efficient investor by giving him a lower number of stakes in a more valuable company.

Credibility

We have already seen that in a variety of circumstances governments are unable to commit to future policy, and investors' uncertainty about a government's preferences can dramatically affect the economic success of privatization. Indeed, outside investors have to be reassured that they will not be expropriated *ex post* by populist politicians who might interfere in the operating activities of the company to reallocate value to insiders.

Perotti (1995) shows how privatization can be designed to make market-oriented policies credible. Suppose first that there are two possible types of government: a government which is truly committed not to interfere, and a populist government which cannot resist expropriating investors after the sale.

In the initial period, privatization occurs and governments decide the size of the first stake sold. Importantly, it is assumed that the first tranche involves the transfer of control, independently of the size of the stake. Then production takes place and governments decide whether to redistribute value or not. Redistribution takes the form of an exogenous transfer to the government's preferred constituency financed by expropriation of a fraction of profits. In the second period, governments privatize the second tranche, then production and redistribution occur.

As in other models, privatization improves efficiency so that the manager exerts effort and profits are realized, whereas under state ownership incentives are weak and the company profits are zero.

When there is no uncertainty over government preferences, it is easy to show that both types of government maximize their utility with an immediate and complete sale. In both cases the manager's effort and company's profits are an increasing function of the stake sold. Obviously, the net value of the firm will be lower when the divesting government is populist, as the *ex post* interference will negatively affect the manager's incentives to invest.

Suppose instead that the government's preferences are private information. *Ex ante* any policy announcement would not be credible as a populist government has incentives to mimic the market oriented government in order to maximize revenue. If investors must form expectations about the type of issuer they face, full privatization may not be any longer optimal as the stake sold affects the posterior beliefs. Indeed, a small initial stake, while reducing incentives, signals a willingness to bear a larger fraction of redistribution costs. Clearly, only a committed government has incentives to do so, knowing that interference will not actually occur. Perotti (1995) formalizes this intuition, showing that it exists as a separating equilibrium associated with a critical value of the first stake which signals commitment. At equilibrium, the committed government will sell this stake, while the populist government will sell the entire capital.

However, this result hinges upon a fundamental assumption, that the first tranche always entails the transfer of control independently of the size of the stake sold. This assumption is certainly unsatisfactory as minority sale typically leaves control structures unaffected. If the sale of a large stake is needed to relinquish control, then governments need an additional policy instrument to signal commitment through risk bearing. Perotti shows that strategic underpricing may serve this purpose. By selling the first tranche at a discount, the committed government signals its patience to garner the benefits of privatization over time. On the contrary, the populist government will immediately sell the entire capital at market price.

Financial Market Development

A sustained privatization process implemented through public offerings of shares should have first-order effects on improving the most important feature of a financial market: liquidity.

The financial literature has set forth two main theories to explain the role of privatization in boosting liquidity. The first one relies on improved investors' diversification opportunities; the second on the reduction of policy risk and confidence building.

The first theory assumes the existence of positive externalities driven by the listing decision. If the return of an asset is uncorrelated with that of other securities, the initial public offering of that asset increases risk diversification opportunities for investors. However, each entrepreneur bears the full listing costs without internalizing all the benefits from diversification. As a consequence, stock markets can be trapped in a low liquidity–high risk premium equilibrium due to a coordination failure among firms and investors (Pagano 1993). A privatization policy, which exogenously increases the number of IPOs (initial public offerings) by floating state-owned enterprises (SOEs) in the domestic market, can move the equilibrium away from this underdevelopment trap, and boost liquidity.

Subrahmanyam and Titman (1999) identify a related but different channel through which share issue privatization affects liquidity introducing the concept of 'serendipity' (i.e. the extent to which investors may obtain by chance costless but useful information during their day-to-day operations). For example, when examining one firm, an analyst may come across valuable information about another firm. Albeit noisy, this 'serendipitous' information can be aggregated across many investors, and provide a signal that would not be obtained if the firm were not listed. Clearly, the opportunities to profit from serendipitous information are increasing in the number of firms trading publicly. Therefore, as in Pagano (1993), a privatizing government, by letting a large number of SOEs go public, can move the economy to the 'good' equilibrium characterized by higher informational efficiency and liquidity.

The second theory developed by Perotti and Laeven (2002) claims that privatization may impact on market participation and liquidity indirectly through its effect on credibility or policy risk. As we have seen in Section 1.4, politicians have broad discretionary powers over state-owned firms, and can interfere in the operating activities of the firms by allocating resources to their most preferred constituencies. Market oriented politicians may be willing to signal their commitment, but *ex ante* their announcements will not be fully credible. A sustained privatization programme together with consistent market oriented policies can provide this credible signal, build up investors' confidence, and lead to stock market growth and deepening.

1.6. CONCLUSIONS

This survey of the economic theory of privatization allows us to draw the following conclusions. Under competitive conditions, privatized companies tend to outperform SOEs and to generate large efficiency gains. This is mainly due to the dramatic change in incentives that privatization induces in the management of firms. However, when companies must pursue social objectives, usually there is a trade-off between allocative and productive efficiency. Indeed, private ownership provides incentives to save costs, but first–best allocations become more difficult to implement as regulation is an imperfect substitute for public ownership. It is, however, possible to identify precisely the conditions under which privatization may entail a net welfare gain for society.

These strong normative conclusions are appealing and call for a widespread application of privatization policy. However, the transition towards more efficient allocations of resources comes with social costs which can create political backlash and policy reversals.

The pitfalls of divestiture can be partly avoided with carefully designed privatization methods. In general, the best policy seems to be to give to the population at large a stake in the success of the policy itself. In this direction, share issue privatization associated with underpricing appears to be the most appropriate strategy.

2

Privatization Around the World

2.1. INTRODUCTION

The economic theory of privatization, surveyed in Chapter 1, has seldom been tested in a comprehensive cross country empirical analysis.

The first step of our empirical work consists in a preliminary description of the privatization processes in the various regions of the world.[1] In the Introduction we noticed that in the 1977–2001 period privatization experienced an exponential growth until the second half of the 1990s and then started to decline from 1999 onwards (see Figure 1.1). In this chapter we will review its implementation within the main geographic regions, analysing the process in terms of: extent, measured by the number of transactions and their revenues;[2] time frames; choice of privatization methods (public offering or direct placement); the main sectors involved; the stake sold; the opening of capital to foreigners; the existence of golden share mechanisms (the special rights retained by governments after privatization). Within each area, we will highlight the most interesting national experiences according to the criteria by which we evaluate the quantity and quality of privatization around the world.

Naturally, this descriptive analysis does not pretend to be complete, nor does it want to retrace in detail every privatization in each country. It aims rather at providing a framework for highlighting similarities and differences. To avoid too much detailed description we will refer to charts and tables.

The first aggregation of data, referring to the period 1977–2001, provides a breakdown of the privatization processes by main geographic areas, separately examining the number of transactions and revenues.

The international comparison of the number of deals shows that Western Europe has implemented the greatest number of transactions, followed by Central and Eastern Europe and the former Soviet Union, Asia, and Latin America (see Figure 2.1).[3]

---

[1] The sources of these data are *Privatisation International* and *Securities Data Corporation*, two of the most comprehensive sources for data at transaction level (see Appendix 1).

[2] The term 'transaction' can indicate a complete sale of the 100 per cent of stock or a 'tranche'. Stakes in sizeable companies are often sold through a number of successive placements (tranches) because of the financial market's limited absorption capacity and sometimes for strategic reasons (see Chapters 3 and 4). Revenues are expressed in current US$.

[3] Definitions of the different geographical areas can be found in the footnotes at the beginning of the corresponding paragraphs. Only those areas that have privatized public companies are included.

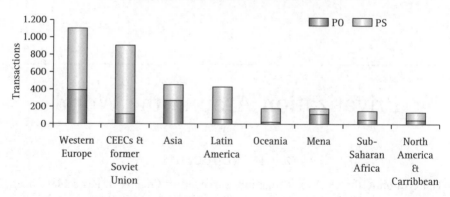

Figure 2.1. *Privatization around the world: ranking by transactions (1977–2001)**
*Definitions of the geographical areas can be found in the footnotes in the text.
Source: Elaboration on *Privatisation International*, and *Securities Data Corporation*.

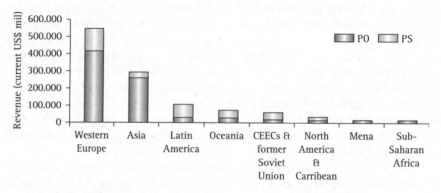

Figure 2.2. *Privatization around the world: ranking by revenue (1977–2001)**
*Definitions of the geographical areas can be found in the footnotes in the text.
Source: Elaboration on *Privatisation International*, and *Securities Data Corporation*.

The breakdown of revenue by geographic areas shows that Western Europe, over the twenty-five year period, accounted for 49 per cent of global revenue, followed by Asia (26 per cent) and Latin America (10 per cent) (see Figure 2.2).

The comparison between the number of deals and revenues offers interesting insights. For example, it demonstrates that privatizations in Central and Eastern Europe and the former Soviet Union were numerous but minor in size. The opposite occurred in Asia.

The data on the privatization methods are surprising. In almost all areas, and even in Western Europe, private sale (henceforth PS), that is a private equity placement to a strategic investor, accounts for the majority of cases. Privatization on public equity markets (public offering, henceforth PO) concerns obviously only major companies.

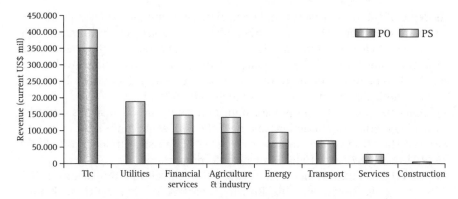

Figure 2.3. *Privatization around the world: revenue by sectors (1977–2001)**
*Definitions of the geographical areas can be found in the footnotes in the text.
Source: Elaboration on *Privatisation International*, and *Securities Data Corporation*.

The breakdown by industry shows that almost no sector is left out of the privatization process and that the greater part of revenue comes from telecommunications, utilities, finance, industrial and agricultural products, and energy (Figure 2.3).[4]

The pre-eminence of Western Europe, which is visible in all the charts, is perhaps due to three factors: (i) the importance of SOEs in Europe (many privatizations occurred because there was a lot to privatize); (ii) the fact that the process began sooner there than in other areas; (iii) the still exceptional weight of the British experience, a phenomenon with unique characteristics not only in terms of the number of deals, but also because of the privatization methods and their results. For these reasons, it is useful to draw out the United Kingdom from the sample group and attempt a comparison between it and other Western European countries.

2.2. THE UNITED KINGDOM

British privatizations account for 19 per cent of the number of transactions and 20 per cent of revenues in Europe. Compared to other regions of the world, the United Kingdom carried out about 6 per cent of global deals, generating 10 per cent of revenue.

The first official documents of the Thatcher government, in large part drafted by the then Chancellor of the Exchequer, Geoffrey Howe, help us to understand

---

[4] Segments are defined as follows. *Agriculture and industry*: agriculture, fishing, and manufacturing industries. *Construction*: construction and public works. *Energy*: petrol drilling and refinery, gas extraction, power generation. *Services*: tourism, hotels, public businesses, other services. *Transport*: airlines, road transport, maritime transport. *Finance*: banks, financial services, insurance services. *Utilities*: airports, ports, urban transport, highways, network railway services, electricity and gas transmission and distribution, postal services, water and sewage services. *Tlc*: Telecommunications.

the logic of the entire process. The immediate goals are the denationalization of companies and the reduction of the public sector borrowing requirement. The fundamental aims are company efficiency, consumer freedom, the liberalization of public monopolies, the development of financial markets and of widespread public shareholding (for more on the theme see Kay, Mayer, and Thompson 1986; Megginson, Nash, and van Randenborgh 1994).

From 1977 onwards, the privatization process in the UK displays a varying dynamic in terms of transactions and revenue, with some concentration in given periods. The effect of the various share issues of British Petroleum (BP), (1977, 1979, 1983, 1987, and 1995) is of notable proportions, as well as the IPO of British Telecommunications (1984), and the block sales of British Gas, British Airways, Rolls Royce, and the British Airport Authority, which took place between 1986 and 1987.

In 1989 the process accelerates due to the sale of utilities/water companies followed by two daunting sales in 1991 (PowerGen and the second tranche of British Telecom).

Until 1991, privatizations took place mainly through public offers of shares. From 1992 onwards, privatizations have involved smaller companies, sometimes owned by local government bodies, sold through private sale. This explains the increase in the number of transactions, and the consequent drop in revenue. From 1994 to 1996, indeed, the process features a higher number of transactions, although revenues do not boast the peaks reported during the second half of the 1980s and in 1991.

The largest number of deals refers to 1996, with the sale of Railtrack accounting for over $3 billion, about 30 per cent of the total revenues raised in that year.

In 1997 the number of transactions fell sharply and the volume of revenues decreased by 88 per cent. After this dip, in 1998 proceeds increased again, with important sales in the energy sector such as the PS of Magnox Electric PLC, accounting for 85 per cent of total revenues. Finally, the last placement of British Telecommunications (previous tranches took place in 1984, 1991, and 1993) brings up the percentage of privatized stock of the company to 100 per cent.

However, by the end of 1997 onwards, the process of divestiture in the UK experiences a scarce number of transactions—with only five deals per year—and low revenue levels, on average around $2.5 billion (Figure 2.4).

British privatizations involve all sectors, but particularly services: utilities and energy sales stand out. Finance has a minor role, mainly because in the UK banks were already in private hands before the big privatization wave.

The analysis of the data relative to the stake sold (see Table 2.1) clearly shows that privatization in the UK is generally complete. The average percentage of stock sold is considerably high in all the sectors involved in the process (81.5 per cent). As we will see, this outcome (achieved through a series of tranches or in a block sale) is typical of the UK, and underlines a willingness to carry out genuine privatizations, in which the ownership and control of companies is transferred to the private sector.

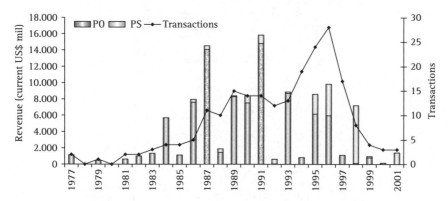

Figure 2.4. *Privatization in the United Kingdom (1977–2001)*
Source: Elaboration on *Privatisation International*, and *Securities Data Corporation*.

However, the British government held, and in some cases continues to hold, a golden share in almost all the main privatized corporations—a special share that gives the state the power of veto over some of the privatized company's strategic decisions. We will tackle the issue in more detail in Chapter 5, where we will discuss the state's control after privatization.

2.3. CONTINENTAL EUROPE

Continental Europe[5] embarks on large-scale privatization in the mid-1980s, especially in France, with the highly politicized privatization of financial institutions by the conservative government elected in 1986, and in Italy with the beginning of the long-lasting process of denationalization of IRI.

The above-mentioned privatization of the French financial sector contributes to record a first peak in revenue in 1987, accounting for 63 per cent of the yearly total amount of proceeds from the area. After a slight dip, the process gathered momentum in 1989 when the governments of Portugal, Spain, Holland, and Sweden adopt a sustained policy of divestiture.

Italy, Portugal, and Turkey reported their first major sales in 1993. Throughout the 1990s privatization also spread out in Belgium, Greece, and Ireland (Wright 1994). In 1999, the process reports a peak in revenue, largely due to the initial public offer (IPO) of Enel in October, and a subsequent private placement of the first Italian Genco in November. As we have noticed before when analysing the UK figures, likewise in Continental European countries, the highest revenues are raised by public offer of shares, as they are typically used

---

[5] In our classification, Continental Europe includes: Andorra, Austria, Belgium, Denmark, Finland, France, Germany, Greece, Iceland, Ireland, Italy, Luxembourg, Malta, Monaco, Netherlands, Norway, Portugal, Spain, Sweden, Switzerland, Turkey. (When referring to Western Europe, the United Kingdom is included.)

Table 2.1. *Average percentage of privatized stock by sector and by privatization method (1977–2001)**

Area	Agriculture & industry			Telecommunications			Energy			Financial services			Transport			Other utilities		
	PO	PS	Average	PO	PS	Average	PO	PS	Average	PO	PS	Average	PO	PS	Average	PO	PS	Average
Western Europe	48	79	63	37	54	46	32	66	49	43	70	56	44	75	59	52	76	64
United Kingdom	–	97	97	63	90	77	48	80	64	45	100	72	100	84	92	81	94	87
CEEC & former Soviet Union	45	56	51	36	49	42	24	47	36	39	58	48	–	62	62	14	57	35
Mena	32	46	39	32	40	36	20	62	41	34	40	37	32	33	33	33	51	42
Sub-Saharan Africa	39	75	57	17	48	32	63	61	62	53	57	55	67	71	69	42	68	55
Asia	31	67	49	26	38	32	25	50	38	29	74	51	26	58	42	32	52	42
Oceania	–	87	87	49	100	75	49	69	59	71	90	81	63	58	60	100	91	96
North America & Caribbean	59	90	74	–	74	74	52	80	66	100	78	89	79	86	82	50	82	66
Latin America	33	81	57	24	80	52	37	74	55	25	77	51	85	75	80	25	75	50

*The average is referred to privatized companies.

Source: Elaboration on *Privatisation International*, and *Securities Data Corporation*.

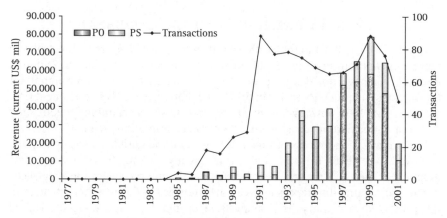

Figure 2.5. *Privatization in Continental Europe (1977–2001)*

Source: Elaboration on *Privatisation International*, and *Securities Data Corporation*.

for larger companies. By the end of 1999, the trend started to decline: in two years the number of privatizations almost halved with a decrease in revenue of about 75 per cent (Figure 2.5).

Agriculture, industry, and the financial sectors have been more heavily privatized at the beginning of the process (with the financial sector leading in terms of proceeds raised). However, from the second half of the 1990s onwards, utilities (and in particular telecommunications) became the core firms involved in the process, accounting for 22 per cent of the deals, and 47 per cent of the global proceeds of the area.

Technically, the goals of European privatization are similar to those of the UK. Up until the first half of the 1990s, however, the breakdown by industry is different, as utilities, electric energy, and telecommunications are still firmly in public hands.

From 1994 onwards, 'strategic' sectors also start to become privatized. Figures on telecommunications are particularly interesting. In 1994 several European countries, such as Spain, Switzerland, Denmark, Finland, and the Netherlands start privatizing telecommunications. Overall, telecommunications represent 68 per cent of the revenue of the utility sector, and 32 per cent of the total proceeds of the area.

The stakes sold are relatively small and suggest some reluctance in relinquishing company control on the part of governments (some governments, such as the French, favouring partial privatization; others, like the German and Italian, simply not giving up control of strategic companies). However, the percentage of stock sold in agriculture, industry and transport, as well as in the utilities in general and financial services sectors are quite considerable.

In parallel with partial sales, statutory constraints are broadly imposed. Often permanent in nature, they underscore the state's difficulty in giving up control and implementing genuine privatization.

2.4. NORTH AMERICA AND THE CARIBBEAN

Between 1978 and 2001 in the North American and Caribbean area,[6] 126 deals are reported, generating lower proceeds with respect to other regions (about $25 billion). Revenue reaches a top value in the 1998–99 period through some important transactions in the energy sector in the United States (such as US Enrichment Co.). By the end of 1999 onwards, however, the process starts declining. In 2001 only five transactions are reported, with a 94 per cent slump in revenue (Figure 2.6).

The privatization process in North America and the Caribbean shows two key features: it is small in scale and varies greatly among the countries' sub-groupings. These differences become obvious if one considers the great economic and cultural differences between the countries of the area. In particular, in the context of a country level analysis, it is important to isolate the United States, where privatization refers mainly to the outsourcing of public services to private operators.

In some cases, private companies sign a contract for the delivery of a public service at regulated tariffs. In others, the government pays the private operator directly for the service. Lopez-de-Silanes, Shleifer, and Vishy (1997) provide a thorough analysis of contracting out in the US. Overall, in the 3,042 counties of the United States, the most frequently privatized services are hospitals, libraries, airports, public transport, aqueducts, gas and electricity supply, fire fighting, prisons, garbage collection, and sewerage.

In the majority of cases, privatization brings significant savings to the tax-payer and the population at large. Private provision of public services tends to involve fewer employees (20 per cent fewer on average) working at higher productivity. For example, official statistics show that in Los Angeles outsourcing has allowed cuts in spending by 36 per cent, with a saving of $250 million for the administration.

Resorting to contracting out appears most marked in those counties belonging to states with severe legislative control over public budgets (i.e. balanced budget previsions, restrictions on debt and bond issues, etc.) and with a history of fiscal crises. Interestingly, available evidence shows that the most efficient and virtuous counties are those with the highest per capita income, low levels of unionization, favourable labour market conditions (mainly low unemployment) and a larger fraction of Republican voters.

Indeed, local politicians with hard budget constraints are forced to privatize public services to achieve greater efficiency. Hard budget constraints exist in the wealthiest and most liberal states, such as California, where the electorates' preferences have been transformed into stringent laws. The opposite happens in the poorer states where levels of unemployment and unionization are high.

---

[6] In our classification, North America and the Caribbean include: Barbados, Belize, British Virgin, Canada, Dominican Republic, Haiti, Honduras, Jamaica, Netherlands Antilles, Nicaragua, St Lucia, Trinidad, Tobago, and the United States.

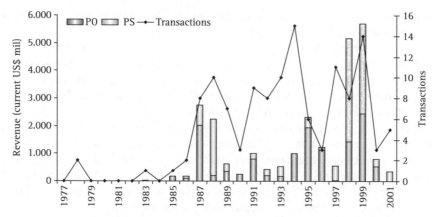

Figure 2.6. *Privatization in North America and the Caribbean (1977–2001)*
Source: Elaboration on *Privatisation International*, and *Securities Data Corporation*.

Turning to our privatization data, the privatization process in the United States begins in 1978 with the sale of Total Petroleum; the United States and Canada have implemented—together—about 78 per cent of total transactions, more than 91 per cent of the global revenue of the entire area.

In more detail, the US (through thirty-eight sales worth $12.2 billion) accounts for 48 per cent of total revenue in the area, basically involving the energy sector, which overall represents 33 per cent of the total amount of proceeds of the country. In the context of US utilities, the Consolidated Rail Corp case is particularly relevant. Conrail, nationalized in 1976, returned to the private sector on 26 March 1987, raising about $1.8 billion. The government has sold all its 85 per cent share at the IPO, and the whole operation represents one of the most significant nationalization and privatization deals by the US government in recent years (Ang and Boyer 2000).

Privatization in Canada also warrants attention. The process starts in 1986, and accounts for 48 per cent of total transactions and 43 per cent of the proceeds, and reaches a first peak in revenue in 1995, with the sales of Petro-Canada, Canadian National Airways, and Edmonton Telephones. After a slow-down in the three subsequent years, in 1999 the country boasts revenues worth $2.3 billion (mainly raised through the sale of Highway 407), and accounting for 21 per cent of the total amount raised since the beginning of the process.

Trinidad and Tobago have implemented some significant deals involving foreign investors in the privatization of BWIA and Power Generation Company.

Jamaica has seen privatization in the agriculture, transport, and telecommunications sectors, selling substantial block stakes to strategic investors. Cable & Wireless holds 59 per cent of Telecommunication of Jamaica, and Telefonica de Espana is one of the strategic investors in Telefonica Larga Distancia di Porto Rico (Wint 1996).

By sector, utilities account for the largest part of deals, followed by the energy and the industrial sectors; thirty-six telecommunications and energy companies have been involved in privatization, raising about $9.2 billion revenue (about 37 per cent of the income for the whole area). The large number of deals in the agriculture and industrial sectors are also noteworthy.

The average percentage of capital sold is around 75 per cent. All privatizations are open to foreign capital and limitations are imposed in only five cases, three of them in telecommunications. The credit sector has the highest average percentage of stock placed, followed by transport, industry, and telecommunications. The lowest average percentage is in the energy sector and in the other utilities. Even here, however, it remains at around 66 per cent.

2.5. LATIN AMERICA

Privatization in Latin America[7] has been important both in terms of figures and economic results (see also Baer and Birch 1994; Ramamurti 1996). As we have already noticed, privatization in the area has been predominantly in the form of direct placement or asset sale.

In a thirteen-year period, 424 sales have been implemented, generating revenue worth over $109 billion. The area ranks fourth in the world in terms of transactions and third in terms of revenue (Figure 2.7).

Three countries in particular have a great bearing on the total number of transactions: Brazil and Argentina account for 37 per cent of the transactions (19 per cent and 18 per cent respectively) and for 60 per cent of total revenue (32 per cent and 28 per cent respectively), while 15 per cent of total revenue comes from Mexico (over $16 billion) with 16 per cent of the sales.

On closer examination, after the start in 1989, the process accelerates from 1991 onwards, reaching a peak in 1992 with forty-two deals and $9 billion approximately. This acceleration is due to the sales of utilities in Argentina (eight transactions in the electricity sector and six in gas distribution, for 35 per cent of the revenue), to the divestiture of firms in the chemical sector in Brazil, and in the financial sector in Mexico (Multibanco Comermex, Banoro, Banco del Centro, Banco International, accounting for 23 per cent of the proceeds raised in 1992).

Between 1993 and 1996 the process slows down in terms of revenue, resuming from 1995 onwards, and reaching a top value in 1997 with seventy-three deals worth $27 billion, mainly raised in the utilities, the telecommunications, and the services sectors. In 1999 proceeds decreased—in only one year—by

---

[7] In our classification, Latin America includes: Argentina, Bolivia, Brazil, Chile, Colombia, Ecuador, El Salvador, Guatemala, Guyana, Mexico, Panama, Paraguay, Peru, Uruguay, and Venezuela.

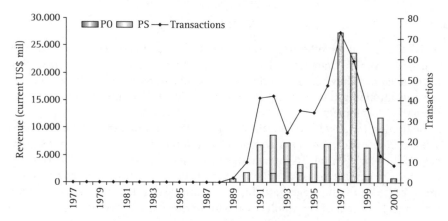

Figure 2.7. *Privatization in Latin America (1977–2001)*

Source: Elaboration on *Privatisation International*, and *Securities Data Corporation*.

almost 75 per cent. By 2001, privatization figures were back to the levels observed at the very beginning of the process in the area.

The breakdown by industry reveals that 45 per cent of the revenue comes from utilities, followed by energy, industry, and credit.

The analysis of the percentages of stock sold yields interesting results (see Table 2.1). The average percentage is around 58 per cent which, considering the absence of the golden share and the openness in most cases to foreign capital, reveals a quite remarkable willingness on the part of governments to transfer property and control to private investors.

Several deals are emblematic of the active role taken by foreign investors. For example, between 1994 and 1997, while British Gas became the key shareholder in Metrogas, Telefonica de Espana bought significant stakes in Peru's CPT and Entel-Peru, while Credit Suisse, Chemical Bank, and Dresdner Bank became strategic investors in Uruguay's Banco Commercial.

With respect to the original British model, these data should make it clear that privatization in Latin America has an additional goal. On top of the traditional objectives, privatization is also a way of attracting foreign capital needed for development and of 'importing' technology through the creation of strategic international partnerships.

For these two reasons, privatization in emerging countries should be seen as a constitutive part of financial liberalization, one in which the savings of industrialized countries (with saturated markets and stable populations with long life expectancies) flow into emerging countries (with high investment deficits and good prospects of profitability, given the population dynamics and the rate of growth of their economies). The same reasoning can be applied to other emerging and less developed countries of the world, beginning with Africa.

2.6. SUB-SAHARAN AFRICA

As is well known, no other region of the world needs investment, infrastructure, and services more than sub-Saharan Africa.[8] Privatization, therefore, has often been called for, above all by international organizations, as an indispensable step towards attracting international investment in SOEs of strategic importance for the area's development.

Beginning in Kenya in 1986, the 146 privatization programmes conducted in sub-Saharan Africa generated almost $7.3 billion of income, only about 0.6 per cent of the world's total. This area ranks last in terms of revenue, and second last in terms of number of transactions. Even in this case, some countries have a great bearing on the aggregate figure. South Africa has raised $2.5 billion (around 34 per cent of the whole area) with fourteen deals, two of which involve an important metals company (Iscor) and a telephone company (Telkom). In the same way, Nigeria's twenty privatizations (about 12 per cent of the total) have a quite marked effect on the total transactions figure (21 per cent) (Figure 2.8).

The sales in the area have occurred mainly within two sub-periods with differences in the methods of privatization. In the period 1988–92 on average transactions are carried out mainly through public offers of sale. The most relevant year of this sub-period is 1989, with the sale of Nigerian Government Southern Oilfields and Iscor, totalling 59 per cent of aggregate revenues of the year. After a dip in 1993, privatization resumes steadily with a net predominance of direct placements. If we exclude Nigeria, the tendency to opt for private negotiation becomes progressively more marked (about 82 per cent of total deals). In 1996 the largest number of transactions is reported, while in 1997 revenue is worth over $2 billion, the highest value of the period. From 1999 onwards, an average revenue of $600 million per year is reported, with a sharp decrease in the number of transactions (from thirteen deals in 1999 to only four operations in 2001).

The manufacturing sector is the most heavily involved in the privatization process. Almost half of the deals are in agriculture and industry, followed by financial institutions, mainly banks, and, to a lesser extent, services, energy, and telecommunications.

The average percentage of stock sold is 55 per cent (see Table 2.1). Combining this figure with the virtual absence of statutory limitations such as the golden share (found almost exclusively in sales, which exhibit different features with respect to the rest of sub-Saharan countries), it can be asserted that governments are quite willing to giving up control of SOEs, above all to foreign investors.

Analysing single operations, stakes bought by foreign companies and institutional investors are significant. For example, in 1995, the Societé des

---

[8] In our classification, sub-Saharan Africa includes: Benin, Cameroon, Chad, Congo, Ethiopia, Gabon, Ghana, Guinea, the Ivory Coast, Kenya, Lesotho, Malawi, Mali, Mauritius, Mozambique, Nigeria, Rwanda, Sao Tome, Senegal, Sierra Leone, South Africa, Sudan, Tanzania, Uganda, Zambia, Zimbabwe.

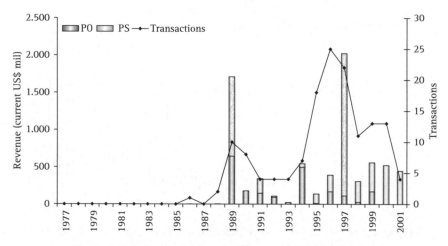

Figure 2.8. *Privatization in sub-Saharan Africa (1977–2001)*

Source: Elaboration on *Privatisation International*, and *Securities Data Corporation*.

Caoutchous de Grand Béreby of the Ivory Coast places 60 per cent of its capital through private negotiation with a consortium led by the Belgian company Socfinal. In the same year, KLM buys a majority holding in Kenya Airways. Foreign investors are also particularly active in telecommunications: France Telecom bought 51 per cent of Telcom (Ivory Coast); Atlantic Telenetwork took 67 per cent of SET (Congo); Telecom Malaysia acquired 60 per cent of Sotelgui (Guinea), later taking substantial stakes in telephone companies in South Africa and Ghana. In other cases, foreign companies are called upon to manage infrastructure concessions, as happened with the railway companies of the Ivory Coast and Burkina Faso.[9]

2.7. THE MIDDLE EAST AND NORTH AFRICA

The privatization process in the Middle East and North Africa (MENA)[10] is also of limited scale (see El-Naggar 1989). The 149 deals implemented have raised only $13.7 billion approximately (Figure 2.9).

Privatization in MENA starts in 1986 in Israel with the manufacturing sector. After a pause in 1990, the process (measured in terms of transactions) progressively accelerates, reaching a peak in 1996. However, important years in terms of revenue raised are 1997 and 1998 due to several sales in the financial

---

[9] This trend was interpreted by some as a renewed interest on the part of local governments in the participation of foreign investors in the privatization process, with the aim of improving efficiency (Laffont and Meleu, 1997). Partial privatization, in other words, allows increased productivity, thanks to strategic partnerships, and as a consequence allows governments in power and their leaders to extract more rents from more efficient firms.

[10] In our classification, the Middle East and North Africa (MENA) include: Algeria, Bahrain, Egypt, Israel, Jordan, Kuwait, Lebanon, Mauritania, Morocco, Oman, Qatar, Tunisia.

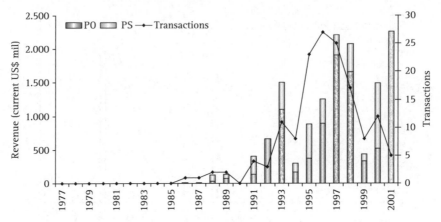

Figure 2.9. *Privatization in the Middle East and North Africa (1977–2001)*
Source: Elaboration on *Privatisation International,* and *Securities Data Corporation.*

sector in Lebanon, Bahrain, and Israel. Interestingly, MENA countries do not feature in the marked global privatization slow-down of 1999–2001. Indeed, revenues have been steadily increasing from 1999 onwards, and in 2001 they are worth almost $2.2 billion, mainly due to the partial privatization of Maroc Telecom (35 per cent of its capital is sold), which accounts for $2 billion.

At a single country level, about 44 per cent of the deals have been carried out by Egypt, obtaining 15 per cent of total proceeds, while Israel, with 25 per cent of total deals, raises 34 per cent of the revenue, mainly in the financial sector.

If we drop Israel—which for a variety of cultural, economic, and political reasons is not comparable to the other nations in the area—revenues are very low and similar to those of sub-Saharan Africa despite the higher level of economic development.

The distribution of deals by sector shows a high percentage of privatization of manufacturing and services companies (above all in tourism) and of the financial institutions: the financial sector, indeed, plays a greater role in terms of the number of transactions and proceeds, accounting for 32 per cent of the deals, worth 39 per cent of total revenues. The analysis of the average percentage of stock sold in the various sectors does not provide any conclusive answer about the government's willingness to relinquish control in strategic vs. non-strategic sectors.

Certain countries deserve particular attention. Egypt, for example, reports the highest number of deals (sixty-five) and appears to be committed to boost the capitalization of its financial market, having opted for the public offer of shares for almost 80 per cent of the companies sold (Tesche and Tohamy 1994). Morocco has conducted some important transactions in the banking sector through direct placements which included some of the most important merchant banks as strategic investors.

2.8. ASIA

Asia is one of the areas most heavily involved in the global privatization process.[11] From 1985 to 2001, the 448 transactions have raised a total revenue worth over $296 billion. This result places Asia in third position in ranking by deals, and in second by revenue, after Western Europe (see Figures 2.1 and 2.2). A first big cluster of deals is observed in the 1986–88 period, exhibiting a peak in proceeds in 1987. However, these figures refer to the privatization of a single company: Nippon Telegraph and Telephone (NTT), the national telecommunications operator of Japan. The first two NTT share offerings were executed between February 1987 and November 1987, the latter representing the largest single private-sector security offer in history (Megginson and Netter 2001). Together with the October 1988 tranche, the first privatization wave on NTT allows the Japanese government to raise almost $80 billion.

After a dip in 1989, the process resumes in the 1991–94 period, basically through some important operations in the telecommunications (Indostat, and Japan Telecom), as well as in the manufacturing sector (Japan Tobacco). The highest number of transactions is reported in 1997, while the largest amount of total proceeds is in 1999, when the fifth tranche of NTT is issued, along with other important transactions in the telecommunications in South Korea (Korea Telecom), and China (China Telecom Hong Kong). Some significant operations are also found in the utilities, in particular the privatization of East Japan Railroads in July 1999 (accounting for almost $6 billion) (Figure 2.10).

By the end of 1999 to 2001 the process had slowed down both in terms of transactions and proceeds.

Japan and China have a great bearing on the data. On the one hand, China accounts for 31 per cent of total deals in the area. On the other, Japan, despite the small number of privatizations, raises almost 63 per cent of the revenue of the region, mainly obtained from the divestiture of the telecommunication sector.

The deals are mainly focused in the manufacturing, services, credit sectors, and utilities. Among utilities, transport and telecommunication infrastructure sales stand out. Transport is at the top of the list in terms of number of deals; telecommunications, however, lead in terms of revenue generated.

The average percentage of stock sold is quite slight (42 per cent), and the percentages of capital sold through public offers of shares are notably lower than those alienated through private placement (see Table 2.1).

All in all, therefore, the Asian process of privatization seems mainly geared to attracting capital to the public sector and foreshadows the tight links between government, banks, and companies.

Chinese privatizations deserve an in-depth examination for special reasons. First, as has already been noted, they account for a large proportion of the deals

---

[11] In our classification, Asia includes: Armenia, Bangladesh, Cambodia, China, India, Indonesia, Japan, South Korea, Malaysia, Pakistan, the Philippines, Singapore, Sri Lanka, Taiwan, Thailand.

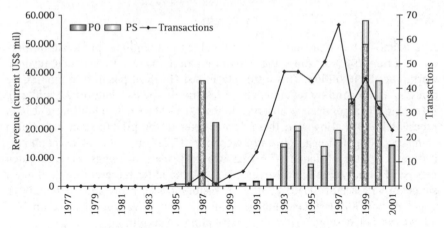

Figure 2.10. *Privatization in Asia (1977–2001)*

Source: Elaboration on *Privatisation International*, and *Securities Data Corporation*.

in the area. Second, they are carried out with distinctive methods of sale (Bolton 1995; Li 1997). The majority of transactions are characterized by the issue of different types of shares: 'Class A' shares which were reserved for national investors and denominated in Chinese currency; and 'Class B' shares issued for foreign investors and denominated in US dollars. In 1994, after a sharp fall in the B index essentially due to the Chinese market's opaqueness, the government opted for flotation on international markets, issuing 'Class N' shares to be placed on the New York stock exchange and 'Class H' shares floated in Hong Kong.

Their flotation on efficient international markets, however, did not prevent a 32 per cent fall in 1995 and a further fall in the B-index 1997 and 1998. Faced with these failures, the Chinese government seems inclined to abandon the idea of sale by class of shares and to allow qualified foreign institutional investors to enter in the domestic capital market.

The Japanese case is, from certain points of view, anomalous. At first sight, Japanese privatization appears a successful experience, given the remarkable revenue generated (over $187 billion) through a small number of deals (eighteen). Closer examination reveals that the success of the first three tranches of the telephone giant NTT coincides with particularly favourable economic conditions and a speculative bubble on the Tokyo market.

Also, it must be noted that control of NTT remains tightly in the government's hands. As of the year 2000, it holds a 53 per cent stake, dwarfing foreign investors, who own a tiny 1 per cent. Later sales, conducted (in 1998, 1999, and 2000) under sluggish economic conditions are not as successful, largely because of ill-considered pricing decisions made without the involvement of international advisers.

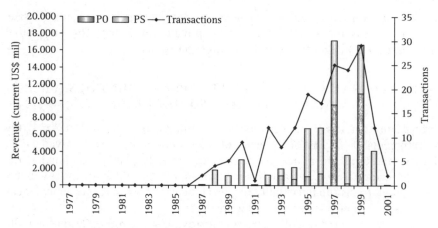

Figure 2.11. *Privatization in Oceania (1977–2001)*

Source: Elaboration on *Privatisation International*, and *Securities Data Corporation*.

2.9. OCEANIA

Oceania, together with sub-Saharan Africa and North America and the Caribbean, shows a limited number of privatizations, although it raises 6 per cent of global revenues (Figure 2.11).[12]

The process marks a sharp acceleration from 1995 with a yearly average of 18 transactions and proceeds worth $8 billion. Year 1997 boasts the top value in revenue due to some significant sales in the utilities and the telecommunications in Australia. From 1999 to 2001 it followed the usual trend and both transactions and proceeds decreased abruptly.

Australia and New Zealand's privatizations are predominantly direct placements. Utilities account for 34 per cent of deals. It is worth noting that although the number of transactions in the manufacturing and services sectors is high, it brings one of the lowest levels of revenue.

The average percentage of capital sold in Oceania is fairly high (76 per cent), and this holds for most sectors reaching a high of 81 per cent in the financial and credit sectors. The picture does not change when we look at the utilities, with percentages in line with the average both in energy and New Zealand's tele-communications (see Table 2.1). In general, the state does not impose limitations or statutory restrictions on privatized companies, apart from the so-called *kiwi share*, which—in some cases—implies tariff regulation in public utilities.

In Australia, privatization begins in competitive sectors such as insurance and banking, then moves on into electricity, gas, and transport infrastructures. Transactions are usually accompanied by massive restructuring measures and

[12] In our classification, Oceania includes: Australia, Fiji, French Polynesia, New Zealand, Papua New Guinea.

regulations. In 1996, a network of twenty-two federal airports are placed on sale, the concessions for which are passed to private companies. This substantial privatization is behind the spike in revenue that year.

2.10. CENTRAL AND EASTERN EUROPEAN COUNTRIES (CEECs) AND THE FORMER SOVIET UNION

Privatisation in transition economies is a unique phenomenon. Even if the governments of the East share many of the general objectives of privatization, initial conditions are radically different. In centrally planned economies, the private sector barely exists and has to be created from scratch. Privatization, for better or worse, is fundamental to the development of a market economy (Sachs 1992; Shleifer and Vishny 1994) (Figure 2.12).

Compared with the rest of the world, the privatizations of East Europe and the former Soviet Union[13] are of considerable size, giving the area second place for number of transactions, with 919 deals, and fifth place for revenue, around $52 billion (see Figures 2.1 and 2.2).

After 1989, Hungary kicks off privatization in the CEECs, maybe due to the presence of a social background suitable to the development of the market economy, which nationalization never managed to eradicate completely. In 1991, Czechoslovakia and Poland join in the process and, in 1992 Romania, Estonia, and Russia follow. The process marks time in a number of countries in 1993. In 1994 and 1995, the first transactions in Croatia and Latvia take place.

Revenues show a peak in 1997, when they account for almost 22 per cent of global proceeds. This acceleration is basically due to the privatization of telecommunications, which account for over 48 per cent of total proceeds; the energy and industrial sectors are worth mentioning, having raised respectively 22 and 15 per cent of the annual income.

After a dramatic fall in 1998 (when the number of transactions decreased by one-third and revenues were cut by more than one half with respect to the previous year), the process boomed in 1999, due to some important transactions in the energy, the telecommunications, and in the financial sectors.

Interestingly, recent data indicate that Central and Eastern Europe and the former Soviet Union's countries are—together with the MENA region—the only areas around the world where privatization continues apace, with a significant number of transactions (sixty-four in 2001), and a noteworthy volume of revenues.

Overall, the sectors most involved in privatization are agriculture and industry, followed by utilities; while finance and credit occupy marginal positions. The

---

[13] In our classification, Central-Eastern Europe and the former Soviet Union include: Albania, Bosnia, Bulgaria, Croatia, the Czech Republic, Czechoslovakia, East Germany, Estonia, Georgia, Hungary, Kazakhstan, Latvia, Lithuania, Macedonia, Moldova, Poland, Romania, Russian Federation, Slovak Republic, Slovenia, Soviet Union, Ukraine, Uzbekistan, Yugoslavia.

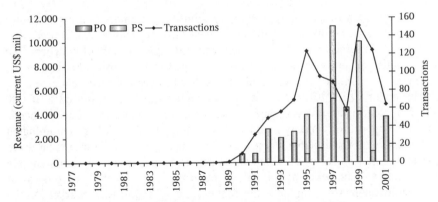

Figure 2.12. *Privatization in Eastern European Countries (CEEC) and the former Soviet Union (1977–2001)*

Source: Elaboration on *Privatisation International*, and *Securities Data Corporation*.

breakdown reveals higher proceeds raised in the strategic sectors of energy and telecommunications.

The percentages of privatized stock are high on average, close to 46 per cent in agriculture, industry, and transport and over 50 per cent in utilities (see Table 2.1).

The methods of sale warrant attention.[14] Companies to be privatized are first transformed into joint stock companies, or rather private companies under state control, with freely transferable equity holdings, and boards enlarge to include the new stakeholders in the company (in Russia, for example, this includes managers, workers, and local authorities) (Goldstein and Gultekin, 1995). In Russia, both managers and employees are offered options for the free sale or acquisition of shares, with the possibility of payment in vouchers or with the company's non-distributed profits.[15]

The participation of foreign players in these privatizations is noteworthy. Hungary manages to attract large sums of foreign capital.[16] Indeed, many sales in the area are typified by the presence of foreign operators in joint-ventures, above all in utilities. Several deals of this kind involved Russian energy giants such as Lukoil, Mosenergo, and Gaszprom. These take place through direct flotation on foreign markets, importing some of the rules of international capital markets and offering investors better protection.

Most sales have taken place through private negotiation, although this should be qualified to include the other modes of sale which are a distinctive feature of privatization in Eastern Europe.

[14] For a thorough examination of the privatization methods in CEECs see also Castater (2002).

[15] On the role of insiders—managers and employees—in privatization and on the efficiency problems stemming from their involvement see Blanchard and Aghion (1996).

[16] It is estimated that 20 per cent of the industrial sector is now in the hands of either strategic or foreign investors.

In all the countries, excluding Hungary, whose capital markets are sufficiently developed, large chunks of capital are placed through 'mass privatization', that is, through the give-away of assets to citizens through a system of vouchers. The main models of mass privatization are developed in Czechoslovakia and in the former Soviet Union and were applied to other Eastern European countries.

The major Czech privatizations are conducted through a procedure of sale aimed at creating an investor class and a financial market *ex novo*. Each citizen is given the opportunity of buying a voucher costing about 35 dollars denominated in points and not negotiable. Possession of a voucher gives the bearer the right to participate in the process of allocation of shares. Shares in the new company are distributed to whomever had asked for them through a centralized process of price adjustment that simulates the functioning of a walrasian market. At the beginning of the process at least two-thirds of the population give their vouchers to private investment funds (between 1990 and 1991 there were at least 600) often controlled by major banks which are only minimally privatized (Shafik 1995).

The mass privatization process chosen in Russia is substantially different. There are many more companies and investors in Russia than in Czechoslovakia, so a centralized process on a national scale is unworkable. Instead, a decentralized system of local level auctions is chosen. Each citizen was given the opportunity to obtain a freely negotiable voucher at the symbolic price of about 25 rubles (10 US cents) with a purchasing power of 10,000 rubles (Boycko, Shleifer, and Vishny 1995). Vouchers could be sold in an extremely liquid market, invested in funds, or individually in shares in one's company and used to participate in auctions for the assignation of stakes in other companies. The absence of rules and of adequate protection for shareholders, however, led to the concentration of ownership in few hands, creating an oligarchy often linked to the political world and organized crime. Thus 'crony capitalism' was born and very grave political, economic, and financial crises followed.

2.11. CONCLUSIONS

The descriptive analysis proposed in this chapter reveals that between the 1980s and the end of the century a big wave of privatization was carried out at a worldwide level with different forms (in terms of methods of sale) and results (in terms of revenue) within the different countries. The variety presented witness the complexity of the privatization process, and the different divestiture patterns chosen by governments around the world. This preliminary picture seems to suggest that initial conditions and goals both matter, and have influenced the privatization methods, the sector chosen, the stakes sold, and the statutory restrictions applied.

In the following chapters we will dwell on the reasons for such differences, providing an analytical framework to interpret this apparent disorder.

3

The Determinants of Privatization

3.1. INTRODUCTION

The picture illustrated in the previous chapter confirms a now accepted fact: the privatization process, which began in the United Kingdom at the end of the 1970s, spread progressively to the main areas of the world, accelerated during the 1990s, and abruptly slowed down at the end of the twentieth century. The roll-back of the state and its bureaucrats from economic activity, nevertheless, took place at very different speeds and in very different ways. The intensity of the phenomenon, measured in terms of revenue, varies greatly in a cross country comparison.

Why do governments privatize? Why do some countries accomplish large-scale privatization programmes, and others never privatize at all? In this chapter, we tackle these issues, focusing on the economic, political, and institutional determinants of privatization, bringing to the data a series of theoretical hypotheses set forth by the literature.

The availability of certain economic, political, and institutional data in some countries forces us to limit the empirical analysis to the same sample of countries examined by La Porta, López-de-Silanes, Shleifer, and Vishny (1997; 1998).[1] This list identifies countries with some non-financial firms with no government ownership traded on their stock exchanges in 1993. The selection of countries is suitable for our purposes: first, we are particularly interested in studying the role of financial markets in shaping privatization processes; second, legal origin indicators are available in the literature only for these countries. The countries chosen cover all geographical areas, with the sole exception of transition economies. Indeed, it will be inappropriate to include them in our analyses due to the fundamental differences in terms of income level, income distribution, political and economic processes (Boycko, Shleifer, and Vishny 1994). Furthermore, the availability of institutional data is very limited and political data more difficult to interpret. The sample covers the 1977–99 period, and accounts for a large proportion of privatization deals (60 per cent of world privatization sales: 2,688 sales) and 93 per cent of world revenues ($1,216 billion).

The analyses presented in this chapter are focused on revenue as an indicator of the extent of the privatization process carried out in a country.

---

[1] The countries are listed in Table 3.1.

Analysing these data, we will seek to investigate whether privatization is simply driven by economic development or affected also by other economic, political, and institutional factors.

Indeed, the quantity of privatization should increase economic wealth, with an inevitable contraction of the state's ownership of productive assets as long as the economy grows. But initial conditions may also matter. Given the inadequacy of the economic and institutional context, in some countries privatization will be more difficult to implement and will therefore remain incomplete.

Let us proceed in order. The chapter begins with a discussion of the link between privatization and economic development, then looks at the role of a government's budget constraints, to study how public finance may bear on the decision to privatize. The analysis then focuses on the role of financial market development in facilitating divestiture, and of political and ideological factors (the preferences of governments). Finally, it takes into account institutional factors, such as a country's legal tradition and political regimes. The various hypotheses are discussed sequentially. Their validity, however, is assessed through a comprehensive econometric analysis.

3.2. PRIVATIZATION AND ECONOMIC DEVELOPMENT

SOEs are virtually non-existent in the United States. The United Kingdom launched the first large-scale privatization programme in the world, followed by the rest of Europe. Latin America, Oceania, and Asia came next. In North Africa, the Middle East, and sub-Saharan Africa the process is just beginning (as of 2001).

On the basis of these aggregate observations, one might think that privatization is the spontaneous and inevitable consequence of economic development, and that its course is largely independent of historical specifics.

In the initial stages of development, only the state can promote the accumulation of capital in infrastructures and in highly capital-intensive industries. Once development is set in motion, the state gradually rolls back from the economy through the privatization process. The Colbert phase[2] is, in other words, followed by the Thatcherite phase—a form of determinism that echoes, at least as far as methods are concerned, the theory of the stages of economic development. If this view were true, a systematic relation between per capita income and privatization should be observed.

Table 3.1 provides a preliminary account of this theory. In this table, countries are ranked by per capita GDP. A simple comparison of the means of total privatization revenues in the two sub-samples of developed and less developed

---

[2] Jean-Baptiste Colbert (1619–83) was one of the most powerful administrators of the French absolutist state. Colbertism is defined as a 'systematic treatment of economic activities imposed from above by the King' (Coleman 1987). Clearly, there are competing theories of economic development. Gerschenkron, for instance, considers relative backwardness as a possible source of future growth as it motivates institutional innovation and the substitution of the absent preconditions of development.

Table 3.1. *Privatization across countries*

This table reports the aggregate figures on privatization in 48 countries for the 1977–2000 period. Countries are ranked by the average GDP per capita (2000 in constant 1995US$) and are classified as 'developed' and 'less developed' using the median value of the variable to split the sample. *DEALS* is the total number of privatizations. *REVENUES* is total revenues (in US$ mil 1995) from total privatizations. Rev/*GDP* is the ratio of total revenues cumulated in the period to 2000GDP (in US$ mil 1995). *STOCK* is the average of the positive values of the yearly weighed average of privatized stock. *PO/DEALS* is the ratio of the number of privatizations by Public Offer to the total number of privatizations.

Country	Deals	Revenues	Rev/GDP	Stock	PO/Deals
Switzerland	6	7,014.30	0.02	0.54	0.50
Japan	17	187,708.40	0.03	0.15	1.00
Denmark	7	3,533.31	0.02	0.66	0.71
Norway	29	7,979.26	0.05	0.64	0.45
Austria	47	9,597.65	0.04	0.65	0.57
Germany	151	77,752.34	0.03	0.79	0.13
Finland	55	18,404.17	0.11	0.59	0.40
USA	38	12,519.94	0.00	0.97	0.34
Sweden	51	18,970.51	0.07	0.77	0.22
Netherlands	28	18,763.94	0.04	0.59	0.39
Belgium	15	6,675.09	0.02	0.53	0.20
France	97	58,633.64	0.03	0.68	0.55
Singapore	25	3,308.30	0.03	0.54	0.64
Ireland	14	5,811.79	0.06	0.64	0.29
Hong Kong	19	11,187.14	0.07	0.49	0.47
Australia	131	58,054.89	0.13	0.93	0.07
Canada	57	11,439.49	0.02	0.81	0.32
UK	215	133,635.28	0.10	0.91	0.33
Italy	113	98,275.28	0.08	0.63	0.38
Spain	88	48,626.92	0.07	0.65	0.34
New Zealand	42	7,697.39	0.11	0.88	0.10
Israel	36	5,379.36	0.05	0.38	0.72
Greece	37	8,005.71	0.06	0.51	0.49
South Korea	20	9,588.22	0.06	0.16	0.95
Portugal	77	26,691.79	0.21	0.52	0.51
Developed Countries avg.	**57**	**34,209.08**	**0.06**	**0.62**	**0.44**
Argentina	77	32,485.16	0.11	0.78	0.17
Uruguay	2	38.08	0.00	0.77	0.00
Chile	24	3,195.35	0.04	0.70	0.38
Malaysia	33	6,622.95	0.06	0.67	0.33
Brazil	76	33,113.27	0.04	0.68	0.22
South Africa	14	2,987.70	0.00	0.59	0.21
Mexico	67	22,055.61	0.06	0.84	0.07
Venezuela	45	11,156.06	0.14	0.82	0.09
Turkey	28	5,636.27	0.03	0.69	0.18
Thailand	24	5,275.78	0.03	0.54	0.63

Table 3.1. (*Cont.*)

Country	Deals	Revenues	Rev/GDP	Stock	PO/Deals
Peru	66	5,265.56	0.09	0.86	0.05
Colombia	16	4,423.53	0.05	0.55	0.19
Jordan	3	590.46	0.07	0.36	0.00
Ecuador	1	44.76	0.00	0.67	0.00
Egypt	64	2,007.02	0.03	0.37	0.80
Philippines	25	4,935.66	0.06	0.57	0.32
Indonesia	16	7,754.26	0.04	0.34	0.81
Sri Lanka	16	312.83	0.02	0.61	0.06
Zimbabwe	6	71.63	0.01	0.56	0.83
Pakistan	14	2,205.00	0.03	0.71	0.07
India	25	2,283.01	0.00	0.43	0.44
Kenya	14	109.41	0.01	0.56	0.43
Nigeria	20	10,478.17	0.33	0.42	0.95
Less developed Countries avg.	29	7,089.02	0.05	0.61	0.31

Source: Elaboration on *Privatisation International, Securities Data Corporation*, and *World Development Indicators* (World Bank 2002).

countries (LDCs) shows that economic development should matter. On average, the value of privatized assets in developed countries is almost five times larger than in LDCs. The data show that many of the poorer countries of our sample (i.e. Kenya, Zimbabwe, Sri Lanka, Ecuador, Jordan, and Uruguay) report total privatization revenues worth less than $1 billion. By the same token, intense privatization effort is found in rich countries such as Japan, Germany, France, the United Kingdom, and Italy.

However, the data on total privatization revenues may be misleading as they may simply be driven by the size of the country. Larger countries have more SOEs to sell, so a simple supply effect may explain a more intense privatization effort. The right data to look at are revenues suitably scaled by GDP.

Again the comparison of average values of revenues to GDP between the two sub-samples confirms the possible role of economic development. However, the picture is quite mixed. We can certainly find examples of poor countries with limited privatization (e.g. India, Zimbabwe, Ecuador, and Uruguay), and of wealthy European countries along with Australia and New Zealand displaying significant revenues. However, there are numerous cases of economically significant privatization programmes implemented in LDCs and emerging countries (Nigeria, Venezuela, and Argentina), and also examples of very limited privatizations among the richest countries of our sample. The cases of USA, Japan, and Switzerland are certainly emblematic in that respect. This mixed evidence calls for a more systematic empirical test, which we will perform at the end of the chapter.

3.3. GOVERNMENTS' BUDGET CONSTRAINTS

In order to investigate the profound reasons behind a country's decision to privatize, governments' budget constraints must be taken into account. Since the time of Adam Smith, in fact, the sale of assets by the Crown has been undertaken to increase efficiency and, consequently, to reduce sovereign debt and deficits.

Since then the issue has not changed much. Privatization remains an important means of curbing state debt and contributes to narrowing deficits (because of lower interest payments on debt and because the state must no longer subsidize loss-making state-owned companies with 'soft' budget constraints). This reasoning has become stringent in a period of history when balanced budgets have become global economic orthodoxy.

As is well known—since the end of the 1970s—in many developed and less developed economies, governments have once more pursued the objective of squaring public finances. Privatization, in this context, has represented a significant part of budgetary adjustment and has often been considered an alternative to spending cuts or tax increases. If on the one hand large public debts call for the sale of public assets, on the other it is not always easy to gauge the beneficial effects of privatization on public finances.[3]

Some sales in developing or transition countries ended with a negative payoff, given that revenues did not provide for the repayment of debts, nor cover severance pay and fees to consultants and advisers. In the majority of cases, however, sales ended up with significant profits. In these cases, the allocation of revenue became an issue.

Some countries, taking into account the non-recurring nature of revenues, have accounted them within the capital account, earmarking them, for example, to special debt amortization funds. This choice, after a considerable political battle, was adopted in Italy in 1993 and taken up in Mexico. France opted for a mixed solution, allocating revenue to a public debt reduction fund, part of which could be accessed for contributions, even in the capital account, to other state companies.

Governments with less foresight (including Germany and many emerging countries) established that revenue could be used to finance current spending.[4] In this case, the effect on public finances is immediate but ephemeral (Guislain 1997). When privatization cuts subsidies to loss-making or inefficient

---

[3] Clearly, in order to establish the net effect of privatization on public finances one has also to consider the opportunity cost of a reduction in the cash flow rights of SOEs by the government. Indeed, the transfer of ownership entails the loss of the future income stream generated by the company, which could be used to finance the budget. If future dividends are appropriately discounted on privatization prices, privatization could theoretically be neutral on public finances. But budgetary shortfalls typically induce risk aversion, so that a certain windfall privatization revenue is often preferred to an uncertain dividend stream.

[4] In Italy, in 1998, during the final months of the Prodi government it was repeatedly proposed that revenue from the privatization of Telecom Italia should be used to finance a development agency for Southern Italy.

companies, which sometimes happens despite privatization, the beneficial effect of the revenue goes with a reduction of future government expenditure.

In Europe, the impulse to privatize stemming from the need to square public finances has been particularly strong, given the deficit and debt targets set out in the Maastricht Treaty.

In Italy, where the debt-to-GDP ratio is particularly high, where interest payments are still very substantial (they were almost out of control in the mid 1980s and at the beginning of the 1990s) and where SOEs, run with particularly lax budgetary practices, absorbed massive resources over the years, budget constraints mattered in the decision to accelerate privatization during the years of financial crisis (Cavazzuti 1996; Macchiati 1996).

The privatization process, which begins in 1985 with the sale of Sirti, Alitalia, and the first tranche of Banca Commerciale Italiana (Siglienti 1996), picks up speed from 1992 onwards, during the serious financial crises faced in the early 1990s by the Amato and Ciampi governments (Ministero del Tesoro 1992). Thanks to the privatizations conducted within a decade, Italy ranks third in the world by total revenue (see Table 3.1), with significant effects on debt reduction. The most important year is 1999 with thirteen operations, including Enel and Autostrade Spa, which together account for $21.5 billion in revenue.

In Germany, the privatization process is more recent and culminates in 2000, the year that registers the third tranche of Deutsche Telekom, and that globally accounts for over $12 billion of revenue. In Spain, the process speeds up in 1995, in precise coincidence with the deterioration of public finances.

Similar factors lie behind privatization in Latin American countries, traditionally saddled with the burden of a huge public and foreign debt. Mexico, after the 1982 crisis, adopted a very significant programme of budgetary adjustment. In this context, privatization plays a significant role in the attraction of foreign capital. The case of Brazil is analogous, from certain points of view, with substantial waves of privatization coinciding with macro-economic and financial crisis. In many Middle Eastern and African countries privatization re-emerged as a policy option between 1997 and 1998, as crude oil prices and corresponding government revenues fell.

To conclude, the tight intertwining of public financial crises and privatization is not surprising: indeed, the sale of public companies is more often imposed by external circumstances rather than freely chosen.

3.4. THE ROLE OF FINANCIAL MARKETS

It is known that financial market development favours a more efficient allocation of resources because it coordinates savings and directs them to the projects with the best prospects of profitability. By doing so, it favours capital accumulation and, eventually, economic growth (Levine and Zervos 1998).

As we have seen in Chapter 1, a fundamental element of financial market development is *liquidity*, the ease with which traders can buy or sell shares, which is even more important than market capitalization (see O'Hara 1995). Liquidity is crucial because it facilitates diversification (Pagano 1993; Levine 1997), information aggregation (Grossman 1976), monitoring of managers (Hölmstrom and Tirole 1993; Jensen and Meckling 1976) and regulation of firms (Faure-Grimaud 2002).

Clearly, if a liquid stock market is operational when privatization sales occur, it will favour the absorption of big issues, increasing the likelihood of privatization of large state monopolies. But stock market liquidity is also a natural candidate for the explanation of the financial success of privatization in terms of proceeds. First, investors require a discount for shares traded in an illiquid market. Second, by facilitating information aggregation, a liquid market allows fuller extraction of a company's market value from private investors. A higher stock market liquidity should be therefore associated with higher privatization revenues.

But how can financial market development be measured? Market capitalization is certainly an important variable to look at. The empirical literature has also set forth several measures for market liquidity. One of the most widely used is the turnover ratio, given by the ratio of the value of trades to total market capitalization.[5]

A large and liquid stock market indeed facilitates divestiture, allowing governments to maximize revenues. The case of the privatization of Nippon Telegraph & Telephone (NTT)–the Japanese telecommunications monopoly–is interesting in that respect. NTT went public in October 1986. The Japanese government sold 12 per cent of stock, yielding $15 billion. During 1987, the stock market boomed, with a 30 per cent increase in capitalization. The government took advantage of a hot market by issuing a second tranche of the same size in November 1997, which boasted revenue worth $40 billion. The secondary offering of NTT is still one of the world's largest share issues in history, with shares priced at ¥ 2,550,000 (Boutchkova and Megginson 2000). Japan's 70 per cent decline in stock market value in the 1989–98 period probably explains the slowing down of privatization in the 1990s, which resumed in 1999 with two NTT sales as Japan rose from the financial crisis.

It is known that hot markets are exceptionally liquid. The Great Bull Market of the 1990s certainly played a role in explaining the privatization boom at the end of the twentieth century. By the same token, falling stock prices have obviously discouraged sales since then. Selling new shares of a partially privatized company at a price lower than the initial public offering price (often set several years before) means forcing initial investors to realize a capital loss and see their ownership stakes diluted. Professional investors have the expertise to cope with this problem by portfolio diversification. Small shareholders, holding a few

---

[5] There are other measures of liquidity, such as the bid-ask spread, or the Amihud index (see Chiesa and Nicodano 2003).

stocks from privatized companies and exposed to these financial risks, may be reluctant to participate in new privatization issues.

3.5. POLITICAL MAJORITIES

Politics may provide an explanation for privatization. Conservative governments and conservative electorates should have greater faith in markets, should limit the presence of the state and its bureaucrats in the economy, and should be sympathetic with the arguments of Adam Smith against the public ownership of productive assets. They should, in a word, privatize.

Naturally, the statistical link between right-wing political majorities and pro-privatization orientation risks being spurious for the obvious reason that a right-wing government is not synonymous with pro-market ideology. In the real world, many right-wing majorities defend or have defended protectionism and state power.

Beyond national anomalies, it is widely maintained that governments supported by liberal and conservative coalitions favour market economies, and therefore privatization, more than leftist governments which are traditionally oriented towards the broadening of the size of government.

The UK example is typical (see Chapter 2). However, the French case is also shaped by partisan politics. At the beginning of the 1980s, the newly elected socialist government undertook a massive nationalization plan involving five industrial firms (Compagnie Générale d'Electricité (CGE), Rhône Poulenc, Saint Gobain, Péchiney, and Thomson Brandt), two financial firms (Paribas and Suez), and thirty-nine banks. Following the electoral defeat of the socialists in 1986, the Conservative government led by Chirac decides to re-privatize thirteen firms and financial institutions. The privatization wave stops with the return to power of the socialists between 1988 and 1992, resuming in 1993 when the socialists lose the presidential elections, and continues under Conservative governments led by Edouard Balladur and Alain Juppé.

Indeed, from the very beginning up to 1997, the French programme is designed and implemented by the right and firmly opposed by the left, external conditions and the institutional setting being substantially the same. Only from 1997 onwards, when privatizations are gaining momentum worldwide, do left majorities led by Lionel Jospin also embark on large-scale divestiture. However, the newly elected Conservative premier Jean-Pierre Raffarin has announced ambitious plans to privatize and downsize large swathes of the public sector.

A second example of privatization strongly backed by conservatives comes from Argentina. The programme has to be largely attributed to the political will of Carlos Menem, a member of the reformist wing of the Peronist Partido Justicialista.

Menem wins the presidential elections in May 1989. Menem launches the privatization programme as part of a wider stabilization package to face the economic downturn which caused serious social turmoil. In 1992, Menem privatizes twenty-two companies, especially in the telecommunications and electricity sector, raising $6.5 billion. In 1995, Menem obtains a second five-year, presidential mandate. The privatization plan continues apace: in 1997 a plan to sell thirty-three national airports is approved.

These examples suggest that partisan politics and political orientation could explain why governments privatize. However, centre-left governments have also embarked on privatization especially when fiscal conditions deteriorate. In Italy, proceeds worth more than $98 billion (the third value in the global ranking by proceeds after the UK and Japan) have been raised almost exclusively by centre-left governments. On a smaller scale, the timing of Danish privatizations has coincided exactly with the tenure of a social-democratic cabinet led by Rasmussen.

The logic that privatization policy is a priori adopted on the grounds of ideological preferences is not completely satisfactory. Indeed, privatization might be a consistent policy also for left-wing governments if revenues are used for redistribution. A quantitative analysis is therefore needed in order to assess more precisely the indications of the role of politics in privatization.

We characterize the governments' political orientations in the sample group.[6] We thereby identify the privatizations implemented by conservative governments around the world. A privatization sale is, therefore, attributed to the 'right' if it is carried out by a government supported by a conservative majority. The average privatization revenues raised in country-years with 'right wing' governments in office is approximately $16 billion, while with the 'centre-left' the average is about $10 billion. However, if we appropriately scale revenues to GDP, the differences appear negligible. A comprehensive empirical analysis is certainly needed for a final test of the partisan dimension of privatization.

3.6. LEGAL ORIGINS

It is a well documented fact that civil law countries–particularly within the French civil law tradition–have a larger SOE sector with respect to common law countries. The average of SOE value-added and SOE investment as a proportion of GDP for common law countries is roughly 11 per cent, in French and German civil law countries it is 15 per cent and 12 per cent respectively.[7] The state is typically an influential blockholder in French civil law countries. Furthermore, interventionist French civil law countries exhibit a relatively low level of government performance so they are presumably running SOEs quite poorly (La Porta, López-de-Silanes, Shleifer, and Vishny 1999*b*). A government in a French civil law country has more SOEs to sell, and owns big stakes in

---

[6] For the methodology of identifying the political orientation of privatizing governments, see Appendix 1.

[7] These figures refer to the sample of 49 countries in La Porta, López-de-Silanes, Shleifer, and Vishny, 1998. Both variables are referred to the period 1978–91 and are taken from World Bank (1995).

unprofitable companies. In principle, the French civil law origin should be associated with large-scale privatization.

However, a large size of government might be an equilibrium outcome. Politicians in French civil law systems are unwilling to relinquish control in SOEs, which is a powerful instrument of redistribution policy. Interestingly, constitutional provisions that restrain the scope of the private sector, granting the state's monopoly in the provision of strategic services, are typical in French civil law countries.

According to the 1946 French Constitution, 'all property and enterprises of which the running has, or acquires, the character of a national public service or of an actual monopoly are to become public property' (Graham and Prosser 1991: 76). Obviously, this provision does not imply the total prohibition of asset disposals by a French government willing to privatize. Nevertheless, it would face more difficulties in implementing fundamental changes. The Italian Constitution (art. 43) also grants special rights to the state in strategic sectors: 'for purpose of general utility the law may reserve in the first instance or transfer, by means of expropriation and payment of compensation, to the state, to public bodies, or to labour or consumer communities, certain undertakings or categories of undertakings operating essential public services, sources of power, or exercising monopolies and invested primarily with a character of general interest'. The Portuguese Constitution declared irreversible the 1974 nationalization, and it had to be amended twice in 1982 and 1989 to allow for privatizations. Outside Europe, the Mexican and the Brazilian constitutions also grant monopoly rights to the state and have been amended in 1990 and 1995 respectively. Similar provisions can be found in Bolivia and Indonesia. Moreover, the constitutions of Benin, Morocco, Senegal, and Togo require the parliamentary approval of privatization law. Conversely, the United Kingdom, Australia, Malaysia, and New Zealand (which are all common law countries), grant governments the power to privatize without the intervention of the legislature (Guislain 1997).

According to this theory and stylized facts, we would therefore expect a lower quantity of privatizations, and lower stakes sold in French civil law countries *in spite of* their big SOE sector.

Different legal traditions are also associated with radically different patterns of investor protection and corporate governance around the world. Common law countries afford extensive legal protection to shareholders and creditors; at the opposite, French civil law countries protect both classes of investors much less. The legal protection of investors also affects corporate governance: widespread ownership is positively correlated with investors' protection so that French civil law countries exhibit a higher ownership concentration and less developed capital markets. Access to external funds—debt or equity—becomes more difficult the weaker the legal protection a country affords to corporate investors (La Porta, López-de-Silanes, Shleifer, and Vishny 1997; 1998).

Investor protection could be an important determinant of a country's privatizations. The market value of a company and consequently its privatization proceeds should be lower where legal protection is poor since there will be a lower demand for privatized equity by minority shareholders. In this context, governments are reluctant to sell big stakes since they know that investors will discount the risk of being expropriated by the managers of privatized firms. As a consequence, privatization remains sporadic and partial.

The German civil law tradition could also be associated with a different pattern of privatization. First, countries belonging to this group are interventionist, having a relatively large SOE sector, but display quite a high government performance (La Porta, López-de-Silanes, Shleifer, and Vishny 1999*b*). If one infers the efficiency of SOEs from the general performance of the state, German civil law countries possibly have fewer incentives to privatize since they are not forced to sell inefficient firms. Second, German civil law countries give creditors solid protection (especially secured creditors), though not shareholders (La Porta, López-de-Silanes, Shleifer, and Vishny, 1998). This differential in terms of legal protection could explain why in these countries—with the exception of Japan—equity markets are on average very small compared to debt markets, and banks are powerful.

To our knowledge, the role of powerful incumbent banks in the privatization process has not been theoretically investigated. One could claim that banks are fearful of stock market development in the aftermath of privatization because stock markets reduce their business. More simply, one could claim that incumbent banks have a vested interest in financing SOEs with soft budget constraints and, consequently, they will thwart privatization.

To summarize, German civil law countries could be associated with a lower quantity of privatization and lower stakes sold since they are not forced to sell inefficient SOEs and since powerful banks oust state sell-offs.

3.7. POLITICAL INSTITUTIONS

Why have some governments pursued a consistent and sustained privatization policy, while in other countries ambitious programmes have been blocked by adverse interest groups? In that respect, institutional factors may affect one country's ability to privatize, and a political economy approach is probably fruitful to shed some light on these issues.

Two specially chosen examples may help in explaining the role of political institutions in privatization.

As we saw in Chapter 2, the UK privatization programme certainly stands out for its consistency and completeness. At the end of the fourth consecutive Conservative legislature, virtually all state owned corporations were sold out, with SOE value added accounting for only a marginal share of GDP (World Bank 1995).[8]

---

[8] HM Treasury still has some holdings in postal and transport services (see www.hm-treasury. gov.uk).

Interestingly, the British privatization programme was fiercely ousted by the trade unions. Between 1985 and 1986, the National Union of Mineworkers went on a two-year strike against the restructuring of the to-be-privatized coal industry. The engineers of BT also called a strike to oppose the major reductions in staff numbers that privatization foresaw. However, the comfortable majority enjoyed by the Conservatives in Parliament allowed them to push back the opposition and to accomplish the announced programme.

Contrary to this, the history of Belgian privatization is fraught with failed attempts. A significant effort to restructure and denationalize the public sector was displayed at the beginning of the 1980s by various weak coalitional governments led by Prime Minister Martens. This attempt was thwarted by the trade unions in 1983, with a general strike lasting several weeks, which forced the government to postpone this first reforming effort.

In 1986, Martens tried to launch an austerity programme which also included privatization. In this direction, a public commission was established to study the rationalization of state-owned enterprises, eventually recommending the partial sale of Sabena, Belgacom, Societé Nationale d'Investissement (SNI), and CGER (Spinnewyn 2000). Again, this programme was deeply rejected even by the coalition members, and did not lead to any actual privatization. At the beginning of the 1990s, the sales recommended by the 1986 public commission were finally launched, amid strong political and social resistance leading to a new wave of strikes by public sector employees.

The worsening of public finance and the urgent need to meet Maastricht convergence criteria called for the implementation of an austerity programme based on fiscal discipline and privatization. In order to overcome the political stalemate that had characterized any previous major stabilization attempt, Prime Minister Deahene in 1995 asked and obtained a special authorization from Parliament to legislate by decree on certain economic matters, including divestiture. Only under this exceptional rule has Belgium been able to float in the stock market a large number of shares of two important SOEs (i.e. Distrigaz and Dexia), to generate in a two-year period three-quarters of total proceeds raised to date (end 2002), and to implement privatization sales despite a wide social protest.

We claim that different political institutions matter, when explaining a country's ability to implement policies with significant distributional consequences, such as privatization. In particular, majoritarian political systems—as opposed to proportional systems—are more likely to privatize. Majoritarian systems are characterized by a set of institutions which tend to reduce the number of veto players, which in turn provides for higher executive stability. On the contrary, consensual or proportional systems tend to disperse decision-making power among different actors, so that executives are weaker and show a higher turnover.

In a majoritarian country, the higher political cohesion in the coalition supporting the executive allows incumbent governments to privatize sooner, and to privatize a larger fraction of the SOE sector, as the constituency of the 'losers' from the policy change is less likely to enjoy bargaining power. On the contrary, in proportional countries the different political actors will hardly reach an agreement on how to distribute the burden of the policy change, so that privatization is delayed by a 'war of attrition' (as in Alesina and Drazen 1991).

In order to lay down a classification for the institutional systems in our sample of countries we refer to the seminal work in comparative political science by Lijphart (1999). In this approach, institutional systems are ordered along a continuum between two ideal models, *majoritarian* and *consensus*. Both models acknowledge the right of the majority to take decisions that bind all other citizens. However, whereas the majoritarian model relies on the bare majority, the consensus model tries to broaden its size by dispersing decision-making power both within and between different institutional bodies, and by increasing the number of veto players.

Based on these theoretical models, Bortolotti and Pinotti (2003) have developed a political-institutional index for established democracies including three components (i) a disproportionality index (the Gallagher index);[9] (ii) the effective number of parties;[10] (iii) an indicator of the type of executive.[11] Given that these components are strongly interrelated, we have standardized the three indexes on the whole sample and then computed their mean, which yields the POLINST variable. Higher values of the political institutional variable are associated with a better fit with the majoritarian model. We would expect to observe some correlation of this variable with the extent of a country's privatization. The results of this empirical test will be described in the next section.

[9] The Gallagher index (1991) is based on the following formula:

$$G = \sum_{i=1}^{N} \sqrt{\frac{1}{2}(v_i - s_i)^2}$$

v_i = votes share obtained by party i
s_i = seats share held by party i
N = total number of parties.

[10] Laakso and Taagepera (1979) provide a methodology to measure the Effective Number of Parties Index (ENP), which parallels the Herfindal concentration index commonly used in industrial economics, and which takes into account parties' 'blackmail' potential. The ENP, in fact, considers one party's parliamentary share instead of market share:

$$ENP = \frac{1}{\sum_{j=1}^{P} s_j^2}$$

s_i = seats share held by party j
P = number of parties represented in the parliament.

[11] The characterization of executive involves its fractionalization (which raises transaction costs within the executive) and its bargaining power with regard to the parliament (which lowers transaction costs in dealing with the legislative power). To take account of both aspects, Lijphart (1999) sets forth an index distinguishing: (i) one-party governments from coalition governments; (ii) minimal coalition cabinets from minority and oversized ones. Minimal coalition cabinets include only parties whose support is necessary to achieve parliamentary majority, while oversized cabinets do not.

3.8. EMPIRICAL RESULTS

The previous sections have identified a set of possible determinants of privatization. To summarize, the arguments that we have presented suggest that the
extent of privatization could be positively associated with:

- economic development (GDP per capita)
- fiscal distress (public debt to GDP ratio)
- financial market development (market capitalization and turnover ratio)
- right-wing government in office
- common law legal origin (as opposed to French and German civil law)
- majoritarian political systems (as opposed to consensual-proportional
  regimes).

Our empirical strategy is as follows. We have assembled first a large panel
data set for the countries listed in Table 3.1 with yearly ratios of revenues to GDP
and the set of economic, political, and institutional explanatory variables listed
above. We have then run several regressions using different specifications and
estimation techniques. The results presented in Table 3.2 are the ones that we
deem more interesting and robust.[12]

Our Tobit regression shows clearly that privatization is related to high per
capita income, developed financial markets, high levels of sovereign debt, and a
right-wing government in office.

The positive and highly statistically significant coefficient on per capita GDP
indicates that privatization characterizes on average a more advanced stage of
economic development. This evidence partly supports the above mentioned
theory about the role of the state in economic development. In the early stages,
the state can promote capital accumulation, especially in infrastructure. As long
as the economy grows and markets develop, governments may reduce the scope
of their direct ownership, and focus on regulation and redistributive policies.

The empirical analysis shows that high levels of sovereign debt induce governments to privatize, confirming the role of public finance in SOE divestiture stated
in Section 3.3. The coefficient of the debt-to-GDP (*DEBT*)[13] ratio is always significant in several specifications. Privatizing governments are typically
encumbered by debt. And windfall privatization revenues are allocated to
improve (directly and indirectly) fiscal conditions.

The role of financial development is particularly striking: the coefficients of
the capitalization (*CAP*) and the turnover ratio (*TURNOVER*) are always positive and

---

[12] Total revenue to *GDP* is left censored for all the country-years when no privatization occurred,
which are a significant fraction of our sample. Thus, in this case, conventional regression methods fail
to account for the qualitative difference between limit (zero) observations and non-limit (continuous)
observations. To face this data problem, we have performed Tobit analysis, which is based on a new
random variable that infers the missing tail in the distribution of the observed variable, allowing for
estimation by conventional maximum likelihood methods (Amemiya 1985).

[13] In the empirical analysis, the debt ratio has been appropriately lagged on one year to avoid
endogeneity problems. The same applies to our measures of financial market development.

Table 3.2. *Privatization revenue/GDP (around the world, 1977–1999: Tobit)*

This table reports the estimated coefficients and associated standard errors (in parenthesis) of Tobit estimation. The dependent variable REVENUES/GDP is given by the ratio of total revenues from privatization to Gross Domestic Product in country i in year t. The suffix $(t-1)$ indicates that the variable is lagged for one year. The dependent variable is left censored in 0 for the years in which no privatization occurred. Normality of the individual effects is assumed (random-effects model). Wald χ^2 tests the null of joint significance of the parameters. a, b, c denote statistical significance at 1, 5, and 10 per cent level, respectively.

Independent variables	[1]	[2]	[3]
CONSTANT	−0.0199422[a]	−0.0153667[a]	−0.0188275[a]
	(0.0028529)	(0.00020289)	(0.0032131)
GDP PER CAPITA	3.18e–07[a]	2.42e–07[a]	3.81e–07[a]
	(1.11e–07)	(7.26e–08)	(1.50e–07)
GROWTH$_{(t-1)}$	0.0003482[c]	0.0002499[c]	0.0003691[c]
	(0.0001962)	(0.0001826)	(0.0001974)
DEBT$_{(t-1)}$	0.000046[b]	0.0000299[b]	0.0000486[a]
	(0.000194)	(0.000014)	(0.000018)
TURNOVER$_{(t-1)}$	0.0071592[a]	0.0078359[a]	0.007914[a]
	(0.0017616)	(0.0015768)	(0.0017598)
CAP$_{(t-1)}$	0.0086639[a]	0.0066858[a]	0.0082735[a]
	(0.0016048)	(0.0014226)	(0.0017888)
FRENCH LAW	−	0.0015982	0.0017198
		(0.0014923)	(0.0030807)
GERMAN LAW	−	−0.0100961[a]	−0.0134302[b]
		(0.0026622)	(0.0055661)
SCANDINAVIAN LAW	−	−0.0001663	−0.0030482
		(0.0029751)	(0.010363)
RIGHT	−	−	0.0034807[b]
			(0.0014834)
NONDEM	−	−	−0.0081726[a]
			(0.0032131)
No. observations	652	652	652
Uncensored	261	261	261
Left censored	386	386	386
Log likelihood	−2283.5628	−2305.1147	−2273.9536
Wald χ^2	75.92	75.99	85.43

Source: Fondazione Eni Enrico Mattei.

statistically significant at the 1 per cent level. The theoretical prediction about the role of market liquidity in privatization stated in Section 3.4 is largely confirmed in our data. Privatization waves are associated with high market liquidity. Governments take advantage of hot markets, supplying shares of privatized companies when there is excess demand, which in turn fetches a better price.

As to the political dimension of privatization, the coefficient of the dummy RIGHT is positive and statistically significant at the 5 per cent level. Privatization around the world seems shaped by partisan politics, with right-wing governments on average more inclined to divestiture. However, we think that a more proper test of the partisan dimension of privatization should be carried out in the context of wealthy and established democracies.

Interestingly, our empirical results also allow us to explain why governments do not privatize, or more precisely, why some countries are less involved in the process. A first element we single out is the soundness of the political and institutional system: privatization tends to be more limited in scale where democratic political institutions are not in place.[14] Indeed, political accountability is a typical component of country risk. And if investors are wary of being expropriated, the shares of SOE issued by non-democratic governments will be heavily discounted. In turn, this reduces the feasibility of the privatization programme, and the revenue raised.

A second obstacle to large-scale privatization relates to legal tradition. The German civil law tradition negatively and significantly affects the extent of privatization. German law countries such as Austria, Germany, Japan, South Korea, Switzerland, and Taiwan seem particularly reluctant to privatize as opposed to common law countries, which we use as the benchmark. German law is associated with a relatively efficient SOE sector, and with strong banks. The first factor lowers the incentives to privatize; the second reduces the feasibility of a privatization programme, as entrenched financial intermediaries have an interest in financing a relatively profitable SOE sector.

In Section 3.5 we pointed out the possible role of political regimes in privatization. On the one hand, we have majoritarian systems characterized by a marked bi-polarism and executive stability. On the other, we have consensual democracies with strongly proportional electoral rules, and characterized by veto power by minorities. However, comparative political science maintains that these two polar models (and all the various political regimes encompassed within these two extreme cases) can only be applied to advanced democracies.

According to this literature, we will assess the empirical validity of our hypotheses on the role of political institutions in the sub-sample of OECD economies. A selection of the most interesting results obtained from this test is presented in Table 3.3.

A striking result of the analysis conducted in this sub-sample is that our POLINST indicator is strongly related to a country's extent of privatization. The results survive when we control for a continuous measure of the political orientation of government (PARTISAN),[15] for the electoral year, and for past

[14] It is worth noting that these results survive when we control for spurious correlation by use of per capita GDP. Indeed, the dummy NONDEM is always statistically significant at 1 per cent level.

[15] The PARTISAN index is constructed as follows. First, we have located each party entering in the ruling coalition (not to the coalition as a whole) on a left–right scale of political orientation; assigned a score; second, we have weighted the relative importance of each party within the coalition in terms

Table 3.3. *Privatization revenue/GDP (OECD countries, 1977–1999: Tobit)*

This table reports the estimated coefficients and associated standard errors (in parenthesis) of Tobit estimation. The dependent variable REV/GDP is given by the ratio of total revenues from privatization to Gross Domestic Product in country i in year t. The suffix $(t-1)$ indicates that the variable is lagged for one year. The dependent variable is left censored in 0 for the years in which no privatization occurred. Normality of the individual effects is assumed (random-effects model). Wald χ^2 tests the null of joint significance of the parameters. a, b, c denote statistical significance at 1, 5, and 10 per cent level, respectively.

Independent variables	[1]	[2]	[3]	[4]
CONSTANT	−0.02515[a]	−0.02849[a]	−0.03147[a]	−0.03106[a]
	(0.00325)	(0.00370)	(0.00460)	(0.00460)
GDP PER CAPITA	4.06e-07[a]	5.14e-07[a]	5.28e-07[a]	5.25e-07[a]
	(1.13e-07)	(1.22e-07)	(1.20e-07)	(1.20e-07)
GROWTH$_{(t-1)}$	−0.00065[b]	−0.00073[b]	−0.00068[b]	−0.00069[b]
	(0.00029)	(0.00029)	(0.00029)	(0.00029)
DEBT$_{(t-1)}$	0.02568[a]	0.02826[a]	0.02825[a]	0.02813[a]
	(0.00306)	(0.00301)	(0.00300)	(0.00299)
TURNOVER$_{(t-1)}$	-0.00443[a]	0.00491[a]	0.00496[a]	0.00478[a]
	(0.00168)	(0.00157)	(0.00158)	(0.00159)
CAP$_{(t-1)}$	0.01007[a]	0.00893[a]	0.00875[a]	0.00885[a]
	(0.00179)	(0.00175)	(0.00175)	(0.00175)
POLINST	−	0.00138[b]	0.00128[c]	0.00124[c]
		(0.00067)	(0.00067)	(0.00067)
PARTISAN	−	−	0.00046	0.00046
			(0.00042)	(0.00042)
ELECTION	−	−	−	−0.00098
				(0.00117)
No. observations	325	325	325	325
Uncensored	173	173	173	173
Left censored	152	152	152	152
Log likelihood	518.00	520.11	520.69	521.05
Wald χ^2	136.44[a]	132.68[a]	135.48[a]	136.59[a]

Source: Fondazione Eni Enrico Mattei.

privatization revenue (PASTREV). Indeed, majoritarian political institutions appear as one of the more powerful variables to explain why privatization takes place in advanced economies.

As Table 3.3 shows, the results obtained on other economic variables included as regressors are consistent with the findings in the whole sample: economic development, financial market development, and fiscal conditions are still very

of parliamentary seats. For more details on the methodology and sources used, see Appendix 1, Data and Methodology.

relevant. Political orientation does not seem to matter: the PARTISAN index is always positive, but insignificant. This new evidence is quite important, as it indicates that privatization in the OECD started with strong ideological motivation by the UK, but then became progressively bi-partisan policy.

3.9. CONCLUSIONS

The analysis carried out in this chapter aimed at setting forth some hypotheses and explanations about the plausible determinants of privatization. The main message that can be drawn from the analysis is that privatization is determined by the interplay of long-term economic factors—such as economic development—but is also strongly affected by governments' budget constraints, and shaped by political and institutional factors. In more detail, we found that (i) privatization seems to be positively related to economic development, as privatization efforts appear more sustained in developed economies; (ii) squaring public finance is a key rationale, as privatization is found to be systematically associated with high public debt; (iii) hot financial markets favour the sales, which appear concentrated in times of higher liquidity; (iv) political orientation and political institutions matter in the shaping of privatization policies, and in particular right-wing (pro-market) governments, and majoritarian political systems make privatization more likely; (v) finally, legal traditions also matter, as German civil law countries tend to privatize less than common law countries. Due to this complexity, it becomes clear that only a comprehensive approach can provide fruitful insights into a government's decision to privatize.

4

How do Governments Privatize?

4.1. INTRODUCTION

The previous chapter clarified that, while following a common trend, the extent of privatization varies greatly across countries, and that political, economic, and institutional factors have shaped the process over time. The analysis has also shown that privatization involves the balancing of (sometimes) conflicting objectives in a context where economic and institutional constraints play a major role. For example, a trade-off emerges between the political goal of spreading share ownership and the one of revenue maximization, as under-pricing is often necessary to tap domestic retail investors, and even more so where capital markets are not well developed. The same trade-off exists when governments resort to privatization in order to build investors' confidence and gain credibility.

How do governments design privatization to achieve these conflicting objectives? In other words, how do they deal with these trade-offs in the choice of privatization method? Finally, have these methods been useful to target the declared goals?

When governments are confronted with the design of privatization, several issues have to be addressed. The first one is the size of the stake. Governments may decide to relinquish control rapidly, or to proceed gradually with a sequence of issues. A second (and related) problem is whether to raise funds in public or private capital markets. Public equity markets are used for the flotation of larger companies, while private placements are typically chosen for the transfer of control blocks, or when stock markets are weak. Another key issue is the international profile of the sale. As to privatization in public capital markets, governments may opt either for an international/global offering, or for a purely domestic issue. As far as asset sales are concerned, they could decide to open the auction to foreign bidders, or to limit the participation to domestic strategic investors. Finally, the pricing and the allocation of shares among different classes of investors are also very important. Governments may structure the transaction as a fixed-price offering or as a book-building exercise. They may also decide to preferentially allocate discounted shares to managers and employees.[1]

---

[1] For a thorough analysis of privatization techniques see Jones, Megginson, Nash, and Netter (1999); and Ljungqvist, Jenkinson, and Wilhelm (2000).

In what follows, we will focus on some of the main goals of the sales, and explain how a given method can be functional in achieving a specific goal, pointing out the possible trade-offs that any choice involves. The goals that we will analyse in close detail are the widening of share ownership for political reasons, confidence building, and financial market development.

4.2. WIDENING SHARE OWNERSHIP

A first objective affecting the privatization method is the desire to foster popular capitalism and widen share ownership, a goal that right-wing market-oriented governments may find particularly attractive. The reason for this preference is not purely 'ideological', but grounded in self-interest and political opportunism. We have learnt in Chapter 1 that privatization, by making equity investment attractive for the middle classes, can create a constituency with an interest in increasing the value of its assets and therefore be averse to the redistribution policies of the left. In this way, privatization can be a rational strategy for raising the probability of electoral success for liberal–conservative coalitions (Biais and Perotti 2002).

The English experience can be a useful reference point for a first evaluation of this hypothesis. The Thatcher government's privatization programme, especially in the 1983–90 period, was implemented with the declared objective of expanding and spreading equity ownership. This was achieved through a massive programme of share issue privatizations (SIPs) characterized by substantial under-pricing.[2] In this way, the distribution of equity at a discounted price made re-nationalization (proposed in the Labour party's electoral programme)[3] costly and, hence, less likely to find popular support while simultaneously increasing conservative support.[4]

On the eve of the 1987 elections, Norman Tebbit, chair of the Conservative party, wrote to private shareholders of British Telecom warning them of the

---

[2] See Biais and Perotti (2002); and Ljunqvist, Jenkinson, and Wilhelm (2000).

[3] In its 1983 Manifesto, the Labour Party stated that it would 'return to public ownership the public assets and rights hived off by the Tories, with compensation of no more than that received when the assets were denationalised'. On 2 October 1986, the Labour Party Conference approved a policy statement by the National Executive Committee to the effect that a future Labour Government would extend 'social-ownership' in defence and other key British industries, including aerospace, by acquiring or maintaining either full social ownership or a strategic shareholding to establish control in those industries. The statement also said that the Labour Party would not hesitate to acquire a strategic stake in Rolls-Royce and that because Rolls-Royce 'will inevitably require research and other public funding (often for major projects) Labour will require equity participation by the Government in return for the public finance provided' in addition to a strategic stake. A resolution to acquire shares in privatized companies without compensation was rejected.

[4] It may be noted that the political support which is won by strategic underpricing may not be long term, as the small shareholders tend to sell their shares after some time. However, the possibility of a large gain in disposing the shares of privatized firms after the issue could create a political support for the coalition which has implemented the policy (see also Clarke and Pitelis 1993).

eventual dangers and costs of a Labour victory. It is obviously impossible to gauge the importance of this single act to his party's victory in the 1987 election. Data reported by the British Election Survey do show, however, that the larger part of the conservative electorate was made up of new shareholders who out-numbered, by a margin of 10 per cent, voters who had never owned shares.

In truth, there is no sure proof for the argument that, throughout the 1980s and part of the 1990s, privatization in Great Britain has been an essential element of the Conservative party's success. However, privatization might have forced the Labour party to reconsider its political platforms about 'social-ownership' and pick up policies which were fiercely opposed before Mrs Thatcher came to power.

The British experience fits well with the prediction that right-wing governments design privatization to foster popular capitalism. Indeed, the programme has been largely implemented through underpriced share issues in the domestic stock market. In order to verify the empirical validity of this prediction, it is fundamental to extend the analysis to a larger sample of privatization experiences. We would therefore expect privatization implemented by right-wing governments to be structured as public offers (instead of private equity placement), to be strongly underpriced, and to exhibit a preferential allocation of shares towards domestic retail investors.

These empirical predictions seem strongly supported in the data. Bortolotti, Fantini, and Siniscalco (2001) estimate the ratio of privatization by public offer (PO) to the total number of privatization sales in forty-nine countries in the 1977–96 period. As Table 4.1 shows, right-wing governments appear system-atically associated with privatizations on public equity markets, while control-ling for other possible determinants. This analysis confirms that when choosing the privatization method, governments trade off the political benefits of spreading ownership with the opportunity costs of lower proceeds. The results in Table 4.1 clearly indicate that financially distressed governments tend to choose the pri-vate sale method in order to maximize the proceeds and alleviate the public budget. Indeed, the coefficient of the pre-privatization fiscal deficits is negative and significant, especially when we control for the size of the SOE sector and legal origin.

Politically motivated underpricing has been the object of a comprehensive empirical analysis by Jones, Megginson, Nash, and Netter (1999). Using a large sample of international share issue privatizations, they show underpricing to be negatively associated with government expenditures as a percentage of GDP, which can be interpreted as a proxy of 'populism'. Populist governments—as opposed to market oriented governments—appear to be enticed by revenue rather than by the economic benefits of privatization. Importantly, the result is also obtained when controlling for fiscal conditions, which could explain a government's preference for revenue maximization. Fiscal deficits are positively related to underpricing, suggesting that even financially distressed govern-ments may be interested in garnering the long-term economic benefits of

Table 4.1. *Privatization on public equity markets*

The dependent variable PO/SALES is given by the ratio of privatization by public offer (PO) to total sales per country in the period 1977–96. While heteroskedasticity-consistent standard errors are reported in brackets, a, b, and c denote statistical significance at 1, 5, and 10 per cent level, respectively.

Independent variables	[1]	[2]
INTERCEPT	−0.1049	0.1467
	(0.3773)	(0.5012)
LOG OF GNP	0.0249	0.0214
	(0.0309)	(0.0410)
AVGROWTH	0.0529[b]	0.0291
	(0.0222)	(0.0250)
AVDEFICIT	−1.3607	−2.1241[b]
	(0.9223)	(0.8665)
RIGHTGOV	0.2259[b]	0.2452[b]
	(0.1041)	(0.1171)
FRENCH LAW		−0.1813[c]
		(0.1074)
GERMAN LAW		−0.1237
		(0.2390)
SOE		0.0812
		(0.6613)
Adjusted R^2	0.2167	0.2574
No. observations	47	43

Source: Bortolotti, Fantini, and Siniscalco 2001.

privatization.[5] Jones, Megginson, Nash, and Netter (1999) also show that underpricing is affected by income inequality. Higher income inequality implies a poorer median voter enticed by the redistribution policies of the left. Thus, shares must be more strongly underpriced in order to convince him that he should invest.

Another piece of evidence confirming the role of political preferences in explaining privatization methods stems from Bortolotti, Fantini, and Scarpa (2002). An empirical analysis about the international profile of 233 share issue privatizations in twenty OECD countries shows that redistribution concerns are the key. The likelihood of an international offering (i.e. an offering with shares earmarked abroad) is higher in privatization carried out by right-wing market-oriented governments. Interestingly, the number of shares marketed abroad as a percentage of total shares sold is also positively and significantly associated with right-wing governments in office (see Table 4.2).

[5] One might claim that fiscal deficits are instead an endogenous variable with respect to under-pricing, as lower proceeds induce higher deficit. This could introduce a possible bias in the results.

Table 4.2. *Probability of an international share issue privatization (ISIP) and the percentage of shares sold abroad*

This table reports the estimated coefficients and associated t-statistics. Regressions [1], and [3], estimate the probability of an International Share Issue Privatization. Regressions [2], and [4], estimate the number of shares sold abroad as a percentage of total shares sold (*ABROAD*), using the first-stage Probit in sample selection models. The sample selection models I and II use the variable *SIZE/CAP* or the sector dummies, respectively, to identify the equations. *GDP* is per capita Gross Domestic Product in US dollars 1987. *RIGHT* is a political dummy taking the value 1 for liberal-conservative privatizing governments. *DEFICIT* is fiscal deficit to *GDP*. *CREDIBILITY* is the average grades obtained by the country in terms of risk of contract repudiation and risk of expropriation taken from ICRG. *TURNOVER* is the ratio of the volume of trades on the country's stock market to capitalization. *SIZE/CAP* is the ratio of the implied market value of the company to capitalization. IPO is a dummy taking the value 1 when the SIP is an Initial Public Offer. *ENERGY, FINANCE*, and *TLC* are sector dummies. The coefficient σ denotes the standard error of the residuals of the regression equation, and ρ is the correlation coefficient among the residuals of the two regressions. a, b, c denote significance at the 1, 5, or 10 per cent level, respectively.

	Panel A			
Independent variables	Sample selection model I		Sample selection model II	
	Probability of an ISIP [1]	*ABROAD* in ISIPs [2]	Probability of an ISIP [3]	*ABROAD* in ISIPs [4]
CONSTANT	−8.04[a]	0.07	−7.94[a]	−0.20
	(−3.43)	(0.14)	(−3.37)	(−0.44)
GDP PER CAPITA	−0.16E−04	0.22E−06	−0.16E−04	0.87E−06
	(−1.07)	(0.06)	(−1.06)	(0.23)
RIGHT	−0.61[a]	−0.06	−0.62[a]	−0.06[c]
	(−2.81)	(−1.59)	(−2.83)	(−1.76)
DEFICIT	0.06[c]	0.02[a]	0.06[c]	0.02[a]
	(1.83)	(3.69)	(1.82)	(3.68)
CREDIBILITY	0.89[a]	0.04	0.88[a]	0.06
	(3.70)	(0.77)	(3.66)	(1.29)
TURNOVER	1.45[a]	−0.02	1.41[a]	−0.01
	(2.85)	(−0.30)	(2.80)	(−0.18)
ENERGY	0.21	−0.07	0.16	
	(0.57)	(−1.34)	(0.40)	
FINANCE	−0.65[b]	−0.02	−0.67[a]	
	(−2.55)	(−0.43)	(−2.64)	
TLC	0.15	−0.22E−02	0.14	
	(0.37)	(−0.04)	(0.36)	
UTILITY	0.05	−0.06	0.21E−02	
	(0.16)	(−1.20)	(0.73E−02)	
SIZE/CAP	1.46		1.17	0.22
	(0.57)		(0.46)	(0.60)
IPO	−0.10	−0.06[c]	−0.10	−0.06[c]
	(−0.44)	(−1.67)	(−0.43)	(−1.63)
σ		0.20[a]		0.20[a]
		(12.89)		(14.19)

Table 4.2. (Cont.)

Independent variables	Panel A			
	Sample selection model I		Sample selection model II	
	Probability of an ISIP [1]	*ABROAD* in ISIPs [2]	Probability of an ISIP [3]	*ABROAD* in ISIPs [4]
ρ		−0.38		−0.31
		(−1.27)		(−1.00)
Log likelihood		−75.07		−76.44
No. observations		220		220

Source: Bortolotti, Fantini and Scarpa (2002).

This table reports the estimated coefficients and associated t-statistics. Regressions [5], and [7], estimate the probability of an International Share Issue privatization. Regressions [6], and [8] estimate the ratio of shares sold abroad to total shares sold (*ABROAD*) in ISIPs using the first-stage Probit in sample selection models. The sample selection models III and IV use the variable *SIZE/CAP* or the sector dummies, respectively, to identify the equations. *GDP* is per capita Gross Domestic Product in US dollars 1987. *ANTIDIRECTOR* is the measure of shareholder protection by La Porta *et al.* (1998). *CREDIBILITY* is the average grades obtained by the country in terms of risk of contract repudiation and risk of expropriation taken from ICRG. *TURNOVER* is the ratio of the volume of trades on the country's stock market to capitalization. *SIZE/CAP* is the ratio of the implied market value of the company to capitalization. *IPO* is a dummy taking the value 1 when the SIP is an Initial Public Offer. *ENERGY, FINANCE*, and *TLC* are sector dummies. The coefficient σ denotes the standard error of the residuals of the regression equation, and ρ is the correlation coefficient among the residuals of the two regressions. a, b, c denote significance at the 1, 5, or 10 per cent level, respectively.

Independent variables	Panel B			
	Sample selection model III		Sample selection model IV	
	Probability of an ISIP [5]	*ABROAD* in ISIPs [6]	Probability of an ISIP [7]	*ABROAD* in ISIPs [8]
CONSTANT	−5.93[a]	0.40	−5.97[a]	0.18
	(−2.77)	(0.91)	(−2.79)	(0.41)
GDP PER CAPITA	−0.13E−04	0.24E−05	−0.13E−04	−0.20E−05
	(−0.92)	(−0.61)	(−0.92)	(−0.47)
ANTIDIRECTOR	−0.15[c]	−0.05[a]	−0.15[c]	−0.05[a]
	(−1.77)	(−3.37)	(−1.76)	(−3.61)
CREDIBILITY	0.71[a]	0.03[a]	0.72[a]	0.05
	(3.10)	(0.66)	(3.12)	(1.13)
TURNOVER	1.45[a]	−0.05	1.39[a]	−0.04
	(2.88)	(−0.81)	(2.74)	(−0.66)
ENERGY	0.26	−0.04	0.27	
	(0.70)	(−0.71)	(0.68)	
FINANCE	−0.55[b]	−0.01	−0.55[b]	
	(−2.25)	(−0.22)	(−2.24)	
TLC	0.09	−0.01	0.09	
	(0.22)	(−0.21)	(0.24)	

Table 4.2. (*Cont.*)

Independent variables	Panel B			
	Sample selection model III		Sample selection model IV	
	Probability of an ISIP [5]	*ABROAD* in ISIPs [6]	Probability of an ISIP [7]	*ABROAD* in ISIPs [8]
UTILITY	0.09	−0.03	0.07	
	(0.31)	(−0.68)	(0.26)	
SIZE/CAP	1.23		0.95	0.16
	(0.51)		(0.39)	(0.41)
IPO	−0.23	−0.10[a]	−0.22	−0.10[a]
	(−1.08)	(−2.65)	(−1.01)	(−2.89)
σ		0.21[a]		0.20[a]
		(12.91)		(14.59)
ρ		−0.39		−0.26
		(−1.41)		(−0.81)
Log likelihood		−84.71		−85.16
No. observations		220		220

Source: Bortolotti, Fantini and Scarpa (2002).

The analysis provides further support for the fact that a trade-off exists between fostering popular capitalism and revenue generation. Selling shares abroad—which often entails having the company listed on a major and highly liquid foreign exchange—can reduce the cost of capital so that governments can raise more revenue, and also raise the stock market value of the company, which is certainly important for future sales. Indeed, the empirical analysis shows higher fiscal deficit to be significantly related to privatization abroad, both in terms of the probability of observing an international offer and in terms of shares sold to foreign investors.

4.3. CREDIBILITY, COMMITMENT, AND THE STRUCTURE OF THE OFFER

A privatization programme will succeed if it appears credible to national and (most of all to) international investors. This proposition hinges upon the following hypothesis: agents are rational and allocate their savings into profitable businesses with the desired level of risk. The return on investment in a privatized company is influenced by transitory factors, such as discounts at the time of placement, but essentially depends on the soundness of its management, which should be free from political interference in investment decisions and from the risk of expropriation by governments (Schmidt 1996). Credibility, thus defined, depends on the quality of the economic and institutional context as well as on the trustworthiness of the incumbent government.

From a practical viewpoint, acquiring credibility over time—defined by Perotti and Laeven (2002) as *confidence building*—is certainly a difficult task for privatizing governments, as following the right steps is the key to creating positive expectations.[6]

Let us assume that investors have *ex ante* limited information about a government's real commitment to market-oriented policies. In this context, pre-privatization policy announcements cannot be fully credible and investors must form expectations based on the personal reputation of the premier and his economic ministers, and on the consistency of the electoral programmes.

Once the programme of divestiture is set in motion, the government may use its broad discretionary powers to interfere in the operating activity of the company. It can expropriate a part of the profits by raising taxes, revise regulations unexpectedly, or even re-nationalize the company.[7] At the privatization stage investors discount these risks on the price for the shares, with obvious consequences on proceeds. In order to avoid a botched privatization, a government must therefore 'tie its own hands' by adopting measures that would make the opportunistic behaviour just mentioned costly and, subsequently, unlikely.

The decision to choose public offerings and to create widespread share-holdings would be the first of such measures. Indeed, the political costs of an eventual re-nationalization or other actions reducing the value of the investment are higher when the ownership structure of the privatized enterprise is widely dispersed (see Section 4.2).

Sequential sales and price discounts may also serve the same purpose. It is widely documented that the largest privatizations (which typically involve utilities and are affected by the problem of credibility) usually occur through several tranches. The slowness of the process is puzzling in that privatization, in theory, improves efficiency so that a rapid transfer of ownership should be desirable.

A possible explanation of this puzzle comes from the theory commitment by Perotti (1995). A partial sale (i.e. the sale of a minority stake) signals the government's willingness to take on a large part of the risk, as it still owns most of the company's capital.

---

[6] The issue has been extensively studied in the economic literature especially in the area of institutional credibility and commitment in policy making (Schelling 1960; Milgrom and Roberts 1982; Persson and Tabellini 2000).

[7] This event is not completely unlikely. It happened in France in 1981 when the socialist government, under the presidency of Mitterand, issued a nationalization decree concerning two metal-lurgical companies, 36 banks of varying sizes, two financial companies (Suez and Paribas) and five large industrial holding companies: Compagnie Generale d'Electricite (CGE), Saint-Gobain, Pechiney, Rhone-Poulenc, and Thompson-Brandt. Provisions of re-nationalization were threatened many times by the English Labour Party during the electoral campaigns of the 1980s. This is an ever-present risk in many emerging economies. Railtrack, the company controlling Britain's rail infrastructure, represents another interesting case of re-nationalization. Railtrack was privatized in 1997, and floated on the market in the context of deep restructuring of the rail industry. After the turmoil caused by the sequence of crashes and declining share prices, the company was put into administration in 2001, and restructured as a non-profit firm on 3 October 2002.

A committed government knows that as sales progress (and, hence, its reputation consolidates) the success of future privatizations will be enhanced. Spreading sales over time, therefore, is a bet on the consistency of privatization policy. A government that, instead, sells its capital *en bloc* may not seem willing to build up investors' confidence. And from the choice of this privatization method, investors may infer a high probability of future policy reversals.[8]

Underpricing, as well as enticing small shareholders, plays the same strategic role, particularly at the beginning of the process when the sale of minority stakes does not entail any transfer of control. A 'populist' (or not committed) government does not expect to gain credibility over time and, therefore, is not willing to concede any discount at the IPO.

On the basis of these arguments, theory would suggest a process of sale through progressively larger tranches at progressively smaller discounts as long as credibility increases. Empirical evidence partly backs this intuition. Data gathered by Perotti and Guney (1993) on the Thatcher government's privatization programme clearly demonstrate that, initially, the government started with partial sales and opted for block sales only at the end of the programme. Underpricing, at least in the British experience, does not appear to be decreasing over time, as if it were, rather, an intrinsic feature of transactions on public markets.

The predictions set forth in the Perotti model (1995) have been studied in the above mentioned empirical paper by Jones, Megginson, Nash, and Netter (1999), where the percentage sold and underpricing are the two endogenous variables of a structured model encompassing governments' preferences and objectives. The authors show the existence of a positively sloped demand curve with a higher percentage of capital sold correlated with higher underpricing. In the context of low uncertainty about government's preferences, underpricing is unnecessary, and governments signal commitment through partial sales. On the contrary, when uncertainty is high, large stakes sold must be tied to substantial discounts. Importantly, underpricing appears to be strongly affected by a proxy for policy risk, given by the index of economic freedom. The lower the institutional credibility, the higher is the discount needed to convince investors to buy shares.

Credibility also affects the international allocation of shares. However, a diverging pattern is observed in developed and less developed economies. In wealthy countries, lower credibility is associated with privatization in the domestic markets, while in LDCs the opposite occurs. This different behaviour can be interpreted as follows. Government credibility encompasses the risk of

---

[8] Full privatization in a single tranche was chosen for the majority of French privatizations. This was probably due to the urgency of right-wing governments to privatize in an unstable political context. The credibility deficit caused by sale *en bloc* was in part overcome through the *noyaux durs*, that is, substantial stakes held by strategic French investors (Chiri and Panetta 1994). It was not at all plausible that the government 'expropriate' *ex post* the wealth of the country's most influential interest groups.

expropriation of private investment but also a more general assessment of country risk, which refers to the solidity of the rule of law, the presence of social tensions, corruption and the like. In LDCs and emerging countries, the country risk component appears more relevant, and governments resort to international issues to signal the intention to comply with the rules of the international financial community, despite the bad reputation of the home country.[9] In developed economies, this need is less relevant, and more weight is attached to a *government's* credibility in terms of commitment to market oriented policies. Domestic (underpriced) issues aim, indeed, at enhancing credibility, and this explains why governments postpone the sale of shares abroad to a later stage of the programme, when investor confidence is already built. This argument finds strong support in the data, as it holds while controlling for political orientation (see Bortolotti, Fantini, and Scarpa 2002).

4.4. FINANCIAL MARKET DEVELOPMENT

Financial market development is one of the objectives of several privatization programmes around the world, both in developed and emerging economies. For example the UK government stated explicitly that privatization was intended to foster the participation of individual investors in the stock market (Vickers and Yarrow 1988).

Indeed, the promotion of the domestic stock exchange has been a strong financial incentive to divestiture not only in Great Britain, but also in other European countries. Interestingly, the first experiment in recent financial history to foster the participation of individual investors in the stock market through privatization was carried out by Germany in the 1960s under the Adanauer government. This campaign to promote popular capitalism, however, did not succeed, as the German government was forced to bail out disappointed investors, and the population turned out to be reluctant to invest its savings in equity (Esser 1994). The French experience in the mid 1980s is particularly illustrative in that respect. The Chirac government—following the British model—chose to opt for a high-risk strategy by launching a programme of divestiture through large-scale flotation with the objective of revitalizing the Bourse.[10] More recently, the Italian programme for the Stability Pact also included financial market development and the promotion of equity culture as one of the strategic objectives of the privatizations implemented during the 1990s.

In emerging countries, privatization often aimed to create an economic environment favourable to private investment, laying the foundations of capital

---

[9] 'Governments have discovered that privatization through a global equity market placement created an unmatched opportunity to get the attention of investors around the world and to tell the country's story. No investment mission has the impact of a global equity roadshow.' (Shafer, 2000.)

[10] As Dumez and Jeunemaître (1994) point out, the Chirac programme was worth approximately Ffr300 bn, and could produce a 30 per cent increase in the capitalization of the Paris stock market.

market development. For example, the privatization programme in Peru in the 1990–96 period was clearly designed purposely, and foresaw the establishment of a new stock exchange law and the reform of the pension system (Cabello and Shiguiyama 1998). In a similar vein, the Nigerian government promulgated a privatization decree which stated explicitly that the programme aimed at 'increasing the participation of Nigerians in the economic activity through share ownership of productive investments' (Bala 1995). The Chilean programme in the mid 1980s provides another interesting example, as privatization was part of a wider set of reforms designed to rehabilitate the financial system (Laroullet 1995).

More generally, as recently stated by the World Bank, 'a carefully structured and well articulated program for privatising major state-owned entities, combined with efforts to establish a suitable regulatory and legislative framework, can give a stock market the needed boost in size and quality' (Lieberman and Fergusson 1998).

Theoretically, a key question arises. Beyond programmes and announcements, is privatization consistent with the objective of stock market development? And how should government design it to achieve it? Finally, what are the channels—if any—through which a sustained programme improves the size and quality of the financial markets?

Clearly, privatization is not the only policy to foster financial market development. The reduction of tax rates on dividends, the development of an adequate trading infrastructure, the establishment of suitable regulation to ensure information disclosure, good accounting standards, and protection against insider trading are useful measures. Yet a sustained privatization process implemented through public offerings of shares should have first-order effects on improving the most important feature of a financial market: *liquidity*.

If the market is liquid, investors can swiftly alter and better diversify their portfolios, and allocate funds to more profitable investments. This is the reason why stock market liquidity is also important at the aggregate level, as it favours an efficient allocation of resources and fosters long-term growth (Demirguç-Kunt and Levine 1996; Levine and Zervos 1998).

The financial theories summarized in Chapter 1 have clarified why privatization should be the key to domestic financial market development. It is now important to document whether or not the choice of the privatization method is consistent with this stated objective. One would expect privatization of public equity markets to be implemented more frequently in countries where governments are eager to boost domestic financial development. Obviously this choice comes at a cost. As Megginson, Nash, Netter, and Poulsen (2000) point out, if the domestic market is primitive, share issue privatizations are likely to fail, for the simple reason that it is more difficult to find buyers, and that offerings have to be more strongly underpriced (Dewenter and Malatesta 1997). Due to the costs of using the public capital markets, governments may opt for private sales in less developed capital markets.

A comprehensive empirical analysis based on a very large sample of privatizations in developed and less developed countries by Megginson, Nash, Netter, and Poulsen (2000) confirms that the objective of financial market development dominates—on average—revenue maximization. Indeed, share issue privatization is more likely in countries with a lower turnover ratio. This evidence is fully consistent with the empirical results of the international profile of privatization. Interestingly, privatization in the home market—as opposed to the cross-listing abroad—is *again* more likely in countries with a lower turnover ratio. Overall, these results suggest that financial market development is an important objective, and that governments around the world appear particularly eager to achieve it.

4.5. THE POLITICAL AND ECONOMIC CONSEQUENCES OF PRIVATIZATION

In this section we will try to investigate some of the consequences of privatization with respect to the objectives discussed in this chapter. More precisely, we will try to understand whether (i) share issue privatization fosters popular capitalism and creates political support for market oriented platforms; (ii) sustained privatization improves on political risk; (iii) privatization contributes to financial market development.

As to the first objective, there is no strong evidence to show that privatization has contributed to widen share ownership, or to promote popular capitalism, nor that it has significantly shifted political preferences, creating support for market oriented policies.

Boutchkova and Megginson (2000) analyse the evolution of share ownership in a sample of SIPs, concluding that the initial structure of shareholding does not appear to be stable in the long run. Indeed, the striking number of initial shareholders (often over 100,000) declines by 33 per cent within five years of the offering.

The privatization process in the United Kingdom seems to point in the same direction, as the inflation in the number of shareholders in privatized firms has been a temporary phenomenon. Clarke and Pitelis (1993) document that the majority of initial investors quickly disposed of their holdings in order to cash the initial discount, and that the majority of shares ended up with financial institutions. So even in the UK context, where privatization has been explicitly designed to entice small shareholders to achieve political goals, it did not affect the distribution of equity ownership. However, privatization had profound consequences on the development of an equity culture as it introduced the population to the mechanics of share ownership, giving them a (financial) interest in re-electing a Conservative government.

If on the one hand the 'ideological' rationale for divestiture yielded mixed results, sustained privatization has certainly contributed to improving policy risk, allowing governments to gain credibility over time and so building investors' confidence.

Perotti and Van Oijen (2001) and Perotti and Laeven (2002) carry out an empirical analysis on a sample of thirty-one emerging economies, aimed at measuring the changes in policy risk indicators during the privatization process. Their results indicate that sustained privatization seems gradually to strengthen the institutional framework by forcing a resolution of policy and legal uncertainties (which had till then hindered equity market development) and as a consequence, by leading to an improvement in investor confidence.

The effect of privatization on domestic financial market development has been particularly dramatic. A bulk of evidence can be set forth to document the huge impact of privatized companies on several market indicators. Table 4.3 reports the end of period values of the total number of privatized firms relative to the number of listed firms and of the relative market value of privatized firms in OECD economies. Indeed, privatization has largely contributed to boosting domestic market capitalization: even if they account only for 6 per cent of listed firms, privatized companies are worth on average one-fifth of total market value. It is widely known that in several countries, in general the larger companies in the economy are the ones that go through a process of privatization. Among European countries, France, Spain, Portugal, Austria, and Italy exhibit the highest values, ranging from 41 to 83 per cent. Outside Europe, New Zealand ranks in a prominent position, with privatized companies accounting for 30 per cent of the total market value. Conversely, the bare 0.03 per cent found in the USA simply confirms that privatization did not occur in that country.

But probably the most interesting fact emerges from looking at the relative value of the trading in shares of privatized firms. On average, one-quarter of the total trading value is concentrated in privatized stocks. A core group of European countries boasts values ranging from 33 to 61 per cent–certainly remarkable figures.

The monthly series of market values and trading values of privatized firms over the 1985–2000 period presented in Figure 4.1 provides additional support that privatization has contributed to the gradual development of financial markets in many countries. Interestingly, some periods exhibit a very high concentration of trading in privatized stocks, such as Japan in 1993–95, Portugal in 2000, and New Zealand in 1999.

This preliminary evidence provides a rough indication of the role of privatization in financial market development. However, financial development could have happened anyway. For instance, the USA experienced an exponential growth in capitalization and turnover in the 1990s with only limited privatization. The same occurred in Canada, Sweden, Norway, and Germany. So, was privatization really a critical factor in boosting the stock market, or was recent growth driven by financial integration, technological innovation, or de-regulation?

Table 4.3. *The impact of privatization on financial markets*

This table includes the total number of share issue privatization (SIP) in the 1995–2000 period, the end of period (31/12/2000) number of privatized firms as a percentage of the total number of firms quoted on the market, the market capitalization of privatized companies as a percentage of total market capitalization, and the value of trades of privatized firms.

Countries	SIP	Number of privatized firms (%)	Capitalization of privatized firms (%)	Value of trades of privatized firms (%)
Australia	20	2	23	15
Austria	26	23	42	38
Belgium	3	1	10	18
Canada	26	2	5	5
Denmark	6	3	10	14
Finland	22	14	8	9
France	54	6	83	35
Germany	20	2	19	9
Ireland	4	4	12	–
Italy	45	15	41	33
Japan	16	1	6	4
Netherlands	11	3	–	11
New Zealand	7	4	30	48
Norway	13	6	1	0
Portugal	39	35	45	61
Spain	24	2	54	52
Swedan	10	3	10	5
Switzerland	3	1	2	3
United Kingdom	54	2	15	9
United States	7	0	0	0
Average	21	6	22	24

Source: Fondazione Eni Enrico Mattei.

Bortolotti, De Jong, Nicodano, and Schindele (2002) shed light on the issue in a comprehensive analysis of the role of privatization on stock market liquidity in OECD countries, showing that share issue privatization is the key, while accounting for other potential determinants set forth in the literature, such as the enforcement of insider trading regulation, political and country risk, and capital markets liberalization. More precisely, the free float of privatized companies as a share of total capitalization is positively correlated with both the Amihud index and the turnover ratio. SIPs in the energy, telecom, and utility industries also increase both liquidity and turnover. Privatizations in the telecommunications industry–which have been global SIPs–and privatizations combined with the cross-listing of stocks significantly increase domestic liquidity without affecting turnover. Importantly, the improvement in market liquidity is not only due to the higher liquidity of privatized stocks. On the contrary, as the theory suggests,

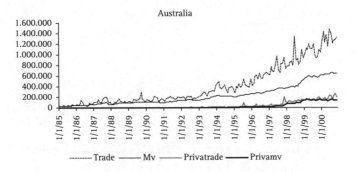

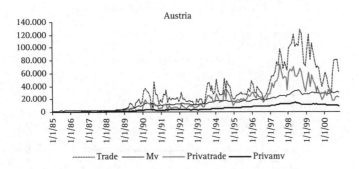

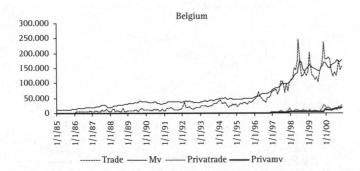

Figure 4.1. *Capitalization and trading value of privatized companies*

Note: We have collected daily series of capitalization and value of trades from a sample of 228 privatized state owned companies (all expressed in local currency) from *Datastream*. We have then built monthly series at the country level for the market value of the privatized firms (*PRIVAMV*) and the total market capitalization (*MV*), as well for the value of trades of privatized firms (*PRIVATRADE*), and the total trade value (*TRADE*). Detailed definitions of these variables can be found in Appendix 1, Data and Methodology.

Source: Elaboration on *Securities Data Corporation*, and *Datastream*.

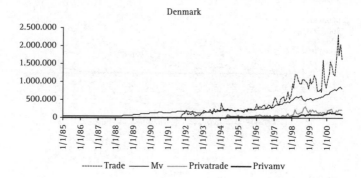

Denmark

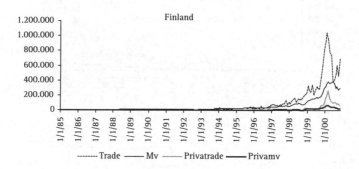

Finland

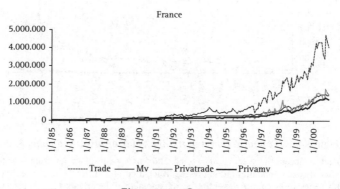

France

Figure 4.1. (*Cont.*)

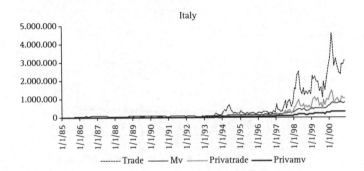

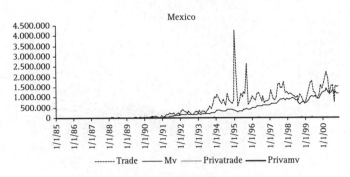

Figure 4.1. (*Cont.*)

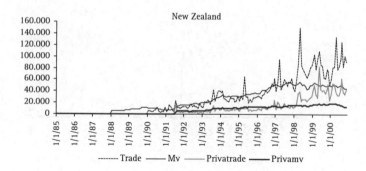

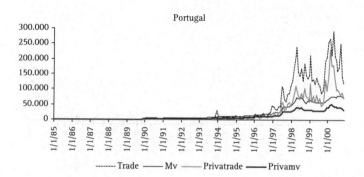

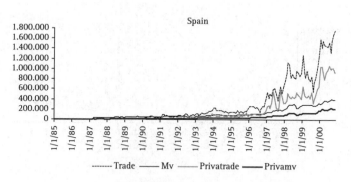

Figure 4.1. (*Cont.*)

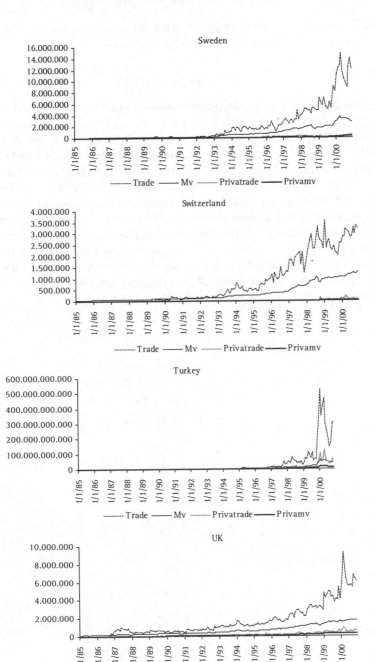

Figure 4.1. (*Cont.*)

a large-scale privatization programme based on SIPs generates important positive externalities on the liquidity of private companies as well.

4.6. CONCLUSIONS

When designing a divestiture programme, governments typically have conflicting objectives which sometimes involve difficult trade-offs. In this chapter we have focused on some of these goals, such as (i) widening share ownership and encouraging popular capitalism; (ii) acquiring credibility over time and building investors' confidence; and finally (iii) promoting domestic financial market development. We have shown that by following the right steps and choosing suitable privatization methods all these objectives can be achieved. The most appropriate policy is a gradual process of sales through underpriced share offerings in the domestic market. The objective of spreading the equity culture in the economy can therefore be consistently pursued through privatization. However, this policy has an opportunity cost in terms of lower revenue raised in the course of the process. Therefore it is less likely to be implemented by short-lived and risk-averse governments, which are often found in the real world.

5

Private Ownership, Public Control

5.1. INTRODUCTION

In the previous chapters we have provided stylized facts about privatization processes, trying to understand why the extent of divestiture varies so greatly across countries. Then we have set forth the main trade-offs that privatization involves, and explained how governments solve these trade-offs through the choice of the privatization method.

This positive analysis has certainly been important and has allowed us to draw a comprehensive picture of the phenomenon at stake. However, a fundamental question remains unexplained: did governments really transfer the ownership and control of SOEs to the private sector? Was privatization aimed at improving incentives in SOEs or simply driven by budgetary motives?

There is a lingering belief that, hidden behind significant results in terms of revenue, either partial sales or majority stakes (sold in combination with legislative and statutory restrictions designed to keep control in the hands of the state) could be found.

This chapter presents updated empirical evidence on the transfer of ownership and control in privatized companies. The transfer of ownership is measured by the stakes sold in the various operations in different countries. The transfer of control, instead, is analysed through the government's residual stake in privatized companies, and by the temporary or permanent restrictions to the control rights of the private investors such as 'golden shares'.

Our analysis allows us to conclude that the large-scale privatization cycle of the 1990s has been important, but incomplete. The process has been largely conducted through partial sales, which have certainly been useful for introducing a monitoring component in the management and for spurring economic performance. However, the state is still an influential blockholder in several privatized firms. Particularly, the state—despite privatization—still controls, by direct and indirect means, large chunks of national strategic sectors, where the larger and most valuable corporations operate.

Several possible factors could explain this reluctance to sell. From the political point of view, governments may want to keep privatized companies under control as it allows them to cater for specific interest groups (Boycko, Shleifer, and Vishny 1994). However, economic and institutional constraints may also hinder the roll-back of the state from economic activity. Indeed, the benefits of full divestiture accrue to a competitive and suitably regulated economy. In this direction, privatization is only one piece of a difficult jigsaw puzzle which requires structural reforms to be completed.

5.2. PARTIAL PRIVATIZATION

The divestiture of minority holdings appears to be a common feature of privatization around the world. From 1977 to 1999, only 47 per cent of the 2,459 deals reported in 121 countries involved the sale of the majority of stock. Interestingly, this percentage shrinks to 30 per cent in the sample of privatization through public offer, where the average size of the stake is 26 per cent. Obviously, these data have to be interpreted carefully. First, the government might have been a minority owner pre-privatization, so the limited size of the stake could simply be ascribed to the fact that the government had few shares to sell. Second, partial privatization could be a snapshot of a process in motion that will end in a complete sale. With this caveat, the size of the stake provides some information about the government's willingness to transfer ownership, and as such warrants systematic attention.

What could be the rationale for a government's decision to sell only minority shareholdings? Is there any economic reason for partial sales or should they be referred solely to the willingness to interfere in SOEs?

A first (obvious) reason is that where fiscal conditions are good, governments have less incentives to privatize, as they do not need revenue to finance the budget. Small stakes sold should then be associated with balanced budgets and lower debt.

However, more subtle explanations can clarify the use of partial sales. First, governments may need to build credibility, and investors' confidence, and subsequently resort to partial sales in order to signal commitment (see Chapter 4, Section 4.3). On the other hand, an already credible government does not need to signal any commitment and will be able to sell larger stakes up front.

Second, investor protection could matter. We already know that where legal protection is poor (as happens in the French civil law countries), governments may be reluctant to sell majority stakes since they know that investors will discount the risk being expropriated by the managers of privatized firms. We also know that legal origin is associated with different structures of corporate governance, and that the German civil law is a good proxy for the presence of strong banks, which could oust privatization (see Chapter 3, Section 3.5). Partial privatization may therefore be observed more often in civil law countries due to the weak protection afforded to small shareholders and to the presence of powerful incumbents opposing divestiture.

Third, well developed financial markets could be functional to complete privatization. Indeed, a large and liquid stock market can absorb larger share issues, so that governments can float a larger percentage of capital. But liquidity matters for more important reasons: a liquid market allows for the monitoring of managers through informative prices and through the threat of takeover, which in turn makes governments willing to sell large stakes, since the shareholders face less risk of expropriation.

It is possible to test these various hypotheses using our international data sets by estimating the percentages of capital sold in each privatization transaction. At this stage, a further crucial distinction between PO (privatizations through public offer) and PS (private sales) has to be made. PS involves smaller companies often privatized fully, and generally under private control after privatization. For the whole sample, the average estimated value of a company—given by the ratio of revenue to the percentage of capital sold, and then multiplied by 100—privatized by PO is $4.5 billion, whereas by PS it is $0.57 billion. The average stake sold by PO is 26 per cent, whereas by PS it is 41 per cent. POs typically involve larger companies, with the consequence that substantial revenue can be raised even through small partial sales. The simple mean therefore overestimates the average amount of stock privatized in a country that has more frequently sold through PS than PO, but raised more revenue by PO than by PS.

To correct this bias, we have constructed *a weighted average percentage of capital sold over all privatized firms*, where the weights are given by the ratios between the revenue from privatization, by PO and PS, and total revenue in country i in year t. We define this variable *wstock*.[1]

Table 5.1 reports the results of Tobit estimation of this variable. It is reassuring to find higher debt strongly related to higher stakes sold, as we know that financial constraints are key drivers in the decision to privatize. Three factors appear more interesting: stock market development, German legal origin, and credibility.

Market capitalization and liquidity (measured by the turnover ratio) is strongly and positively associated with the average stakes sold. Governments are forced to sell minority holdings if the stock market is not sufficiently developed and liquid to absorb big issues or to provide informative prices. Clearly, this does not mean that underdeveloped financial markets make privatization unfeasible, but that governments are forced to gradualism and to stronger underpricing of shares.

Second, full privatization seems particularly difficult to achieve in civil law countries. The German law dummy yields the strongest results, with a negative and highly significant coefficient. This result is particularly striking as it provides further evidence about the possible role of domestic banks in ousting divestiture discovered in the analysis of revenue (see again Chapter 3, Section 3.6). In bank-dominated financial systems, banks may have vested interests in

---

[1] An example would clarify the working of this weighting procedure. In 1999, a country like Italy has privatized 14 companies (6 by PO and 8 by PS) generating $26,586 million in revenue. The average stake sold by PO is 37 per cent, while the one by PS is 68 per cent. The simple mean of privatized stock is 55 per cent. Given that 97 per cent of proceeds were generated by PO, the weighted average is 39.5 per cent. In this way, the average privatized stock is closer to the value that, on average, has generated the largest proportion of revenue.

Private Ownership, Public Control

Table 5.1. *Explaining partial sales*

This table reports the estimated coefficients and associated standard errors (in parenthesis) of Tobit estimation. The dependent variable *WSTOCK* is given by the weighted average percentage of capital sold over all firms where the weights are given by the ratios between the revenues from privatization by PO and PS, and total revenues in country *i* in year *t*. The suffix $(t-1)$ indicates that the variable is lagged for one year. The dependent variable is left censored in 0 for the years in which no privatization occurred. Normality of the individual effects is assumed (random-effects model). Wald χ^2 tests the null of joint significance of the parameters. a, b, and c denote statistical significance at 1, 5, and 10 per cent level, respectively.

Independent variables	[1]	[2]	[3]
CONSTANT	−94.64749[a]	−93.74693[a]	−92.06646[a]
	(12.7073)	(15.64999)	(14.63723)
GDP	0.0020048[a]	0.0028057[a]	0.0022555[a]
	(0.005087)	(0.0004428)	(0.0005879)
$GROWTH_{(t-1)}$	1.597688[b]	1.621441[b]	1.836963[b]
	(8143032)	(0.8094109)	(0.8373524)
$DEBT_{(t-1)}$	0.2720954[a]	0.267592[a]	0.2587366[a]
	(0.0814947)	(0.07943311)	(0.0728266)
$TURNOVER_{(t-1)}$	27.22101[a]	29.3356[a]	29.38696[a]
	(7.175344)	(7.368557)	(7.421176)
$CAP_{(t-1)}$	55.30908[a]	52.77048[a]	49.82898[a]
	(7.702578)	(7.690171)	(7.834967)
FRENCH LAW	−	15.73268	17.01932
		(12.23334)	(13.9385)
GERMAN LAW	−	−41.6645[a]	−44.7987[c]
		(16.16737)	(23.76782)
SCANDINAVIAN LAW	−	−58.7893[a]	−15.93089
		(16.65556)	(19.50013)
RIGHT	−	−	5.644765
			(6.0036)
NONDEM	−	−	−39.07798[a]
			(13.27993)
No. observations	652	652	652
Uncensored	227	227	227
Left censored	409	409	409
Log likelihood	−1,422.2564	−1,419.4915	−1,414.1326
Wald χ^2	117.03	149.06	114.29

Source: Fondazione Eni Enrico Mattei.

financing SOEs as they would lose from a too-rapid switch from debt to equity finance (Hertig 2000). Finally, as predicted by theory, institutional credibility seems to play a major role in explaining partial privatization: lower stakes sold are found in non-democratic contexts. The political dummy 'non-democratic' is attached to countries under authoritarian rule, as dictatorial, military, or one-party regimes, where political competition is absent or extremely limited. These political features apply to some developing and emerging countries in our sample and make investment in privatized companies particularly risky. If the government holds a large block of shares (and consequently privatizes only a minority holding), private shareholders should be reassured, as expropriation would also reduce the value of the investment for the public shareholder. Partial sales appear to be a strategy to signal government willingness to bear residual risk and not to interfere in the operating activity of the company in a context of high policy risk.

The empirical analysis clarifies some of the possible reasons why governments may strategically resort to partial sales. But what are the consequences of this choice?

Although partial sales do not imply a radical change in the control structure, they seem to have significant effects on the financial and operating performance of privatized firms. Gupta (2002) carries out a comprehensive analysis on privatization in India, showing that the level and the growth rates of profitability and labour productivity improve with partial privatization, being negatively and significantly associated with a decrease in government ownership. The privatizations taken into account are truly partial sales, as in the large majority the companies remained tightly controlled by the state after privatization. This feature of the sample allows a proper empirical test of the 'managerial view' about the poor performance of SOEs (Sheshinski and López-Calva 2000). Given that privatization involved the listing of the privatized company shares, the public stock price produced valuable information to monitor managers and alleviate agency problems, even if the company remained under government control.

5.3. THE DYNAMICS OF STATE OWNERSHIP IN PRIVATIZED FIRMS

Partial privatization is certainly an interesting feature of a state's assets disposal. A still unresolved issue is whether partial sales are just a snapshot of a process that will end with complete divestiture, or whether this will not occur in the long term, as if governments were not really intending to give up ownership and control.

Indeed, privatizing the 'first tranche' is a win–win solution. With privatization, governments raise money to finance their budgets, and introduce a monitoring component into management which spurs the performance of their firms. These are the reasons for the first privatizations in France and Italy that juxtaposed public and private shareholders within the capital of large banks and financial sector groups. This model also applies in developing countries where some governments, eager to maintain control over management, preferred to sell minority stakes in many companies, rather than the total capital of few. This is—for example—the case in Nigeria, one of the African countries most involved in the process, where only five of the twenty privatizations involved the divestiture of majority stakes, and the average percentage of capital sold (42 per cent) remains—as of 2001—quite moderate compared to other countries.

The complete divestiture of ownership and relinquishment of control is a more complex and politically costly decision. Obviously, more money can be raised if the company is fully sold off, but by doing so governments lose a powerful instrument for targeted redistribution (as high wages and job security could be earmarked to special categories of workers), the right of having representatives in the boards in order to affect corporate decisions, and the power to safeguard public interests and national security.

In this section, we try to dwell on the issue of government ownership in privatized firms. Clearly, the data to look at are no longer the percentages of capital sold but governments' residual stakes, and possibly their evolution over time.

Data about ultimate ownership are extremely difficult to collect for the entire population of privatized firms. However, by restricting the analysis to OECD countries and to publicly listed firms, shareholdings in privatized SOEs can be found and analysed in detail.

We obtained complete information about shareholdings at the 5 per cent level in 139 privatized firms as of year 2000. We then computed the ultimate (direct and indirect) ownership by private and public shareholders (including the central state, federal or regional bodies, Central Banks, etc.) as the product of cash flow rights along the control chain. This methodology allows us to draw an exhaustive picture of ownership structures in privatized firms, taking into account pyramiding and cross-holdings. We identify three categories of privatized firms according to the identity of the largest ultimate shareholder at the 10 per cent cut-off level: (i) 'state-owned'; (ii) privately owned;[2] (iii) widely held.[3]

Table 5.2 reports some statistics at the country level about ultimate ownership in privatized firms.

For the year 2000, the ownership structure of privatized companies is quite evenly split among our three categories, with a slight predominance of privately owned firms. It is interesting to stress that the 'state-owned' firms (i.e. privatized companies where the state is the largest ultimate shareholder) represent 28 per cent of our sample. Indeed, the privatization process in developed economies is still far from accomplished.

The analysis of the residual stakes yields surprising outcomes. The average stake owned by the public shareholder in 'state-owned' firms is around 37 per cent, while in privately owned it is 32 per cent. 'State-owned' firms show therefore a

---

[2] The type of large private shareholder includes families, unlisted companies, widely held corporations, and widely financial institutions.

[3] A privatized company is defined 'widely held' if the ultimate ownership of the largest shareholder is below 10 per cent.

Table 5.2. *Ultimate ownership in privatized companies*

Country/Year	Privatized companies		'State-owned' companies (%)		Privately owned companies (%)		Widely held companies (%)		Average ultimate ownership in 'state-owned' firms		Average ultimate ownership in privately owned firms	
	2000	1996	2000	1996	2000	1996	2000	1996	2000	1996	2000	1996
Australia	6	6	0.0	0.0	33.3	66.7	66.7	33.3	–	–	77.9	25.5
Austria	11	11	81.8	90.9	18.2	9.1	0.0	0.0	39.5	42.3	49.5	25
Belgium	2	2	50.0	50.0	50.0	50.0	0.0	0.0	23.4	50.0	16.8	16.75
Canada	10	10	20.0	30.0	0.0	20.0	80.0	50.0	14.5	43.3	–	29.45
Denmark	2	2	50.0	100.0	50.0	0.0	0.0	0.0	33.8	63.2	34.4	–
Finland	4	4	100.0	100.0	0.0	0.0	0.0	0.0	48.6	44.3	–	–
France	20	20	20.0	25.0	35.0	40.0	45.0	35.0	37.9	44.0	12.3	19.8
Germany	10	10	40.0	40.0	60.0	60.0	0.0	0.0	48.9	35.9	23.3	19.8
Ireland	2	2	0.0	0.0	100.0	100.0	0.0	0.0	–	–	20.4	11.2
Italy	12	12	33.3	58.3	50.0	8.3	16.7	33.3	40.4	42.9	20.3	64.2
Japan	4	4	50.0	50.0	25.0	50.0	25.0	0.0	59.9	NA	12.5	NA
Mexico	1	1	0.0	0.0	100.0	100.0	0.0	0.0	–	–	49.9	54.8
Netherlands	3	3	33.3	33.3	33.3	33.3	33.3	33.3	34.7	44.0	16.5	6.7
New Zealand	2	2	0.0	0.0	100.0	100.0	0.0	0.0	–	–	57.2	47.7
Norway	6	6	33.3	83.3	17.0	0.0	50.0	16.7	48.8	31.2	98.7	–
Portugal	9	9	33.3	33.3	55.6	55.6	11.0	11.1	27.3	26.0	37.9	35.6
Spain	5	5	20.0	40.0	60.0	20.0	20.0	40.0	51.0	46.4	10.7	27.7
Sweden	3	3	33.0	66.7	0.0	0.0	67.0	33.0	35.3	37.6	–	–
Turkey	3	3	0.0	0.0	100.0	100.0	0.0	0.0	–	–	41.5	41.1
UK	24	24	0.0	0.0	29.0	42.0	70.8	58.3	–	–	18.7	17.4
Total/average	139	139	28.1	37.0	36.7	36.0	35.2	27.0	37.2*	42.4*	32.3*	29.5*

*The average is constructed for countries where data are available for 1996 and 2000.

Source: Fondazione Eni Enrico Mattei.

higher concentration of ownership with respect to privately owned privatized firms.

The high percentages of 'state-owned' firms and the large stakes owned by the public shareholder observed in the year 2000 seem to indicate that privatization has been carried out reluctantly during the 1990s. In order to assess quantitatively this reluctance, we should take a second snapshot in a previous year, and track the evolution of ownership in the post-privatization period up to the year end.

Data availability allows us to go back in time to 1996. A four-year period certainly provides a partial picture of this evolution. However, given that—by construction—all the companies in our sample were privatized no later than 1996, even this relatively short time span is suitable for our purposes.

In 1996, we find a higher number of 'state-owned' firms (37 per cent), a lower number of widely held firms (27 per cent), and about the same number of privately owned companies. The large-scale privatization process of the 1990s (see the Figures in the Introduction and Chapter 2) appears to have two main consequences. First, the state does not any longer play the role of the largest shareholder in several companies (9 per cent of the sample). Second, it contributed to widening share ownership in privatized firms. Indeed, eleven previously state owned companies became widely held firms.[4]

These consequences of the privatization process are certainly relevant. However, as far as ownership structure is concerned, even if some changes are observed in the percentage of 'state-owned' companies, the difference between the average stakes from 1996 to 2000 is only around 5 per cent. Interestingly, the difference between the average stakes held by public and private shareholders shrinks substantially over time, more than halving, from 13 to 5 per cent. This indicates that some dilution of public ownership occurred in privatized companies. Yet the privatization process did not alter considerably the ownership structure of state-owned firms, where governments remain influential block holders.

Ownership structures in developing economies seem to follow a somewhat different pattern of evolution. Boubakri, Cosset, and Guedhami (2001) provide evidence that post-privatization private ownership tends to predominate. This result is consistent with the increase in the stake owned by the largest private shareholder that we find in developed economies. However, they find that privatization results in a relinquishment of control, with a 55 per cent shift in government ownership. While we also document some shift in the percentages of state-owned firms, government ultimate ownership changes only marginally, indicating that privatization did not substantially affect the corporate governance of state controlled firms in advanced economies.

---

[4] However these data have to be interpreted carefully. The state may not rank first any longer in terms of ultimate ownership, due to privatization, but also due to changes in the shareholding of private owners. Indeed, an individual or a company may have acquired stakes from other private shareholders, or in the stock market.

Table 5.3. *Ultimate ownership (UO) in privatized vs. matching (private) firms*

Year	Mean UO of the largest shareholder in privatized firms (a)	Mean UO of the largest shareholder in matching (private) firms (b)	Difference in mean ultimate ownership (a)–(b)	Mean UO of the largest shareholder in 'state-owned' privatized firms (c)	Mean UO of the largest shareholder in private firms matching 'state-owned' privatized firms (d)	Difference in mean ultimate ownership in 'state-owned' firms vs. matching (private) firms (c)–(d)
1996	25.39	17.14	8.25[a] (2.98)	43.66	12.94	30.72[a] (7.75)
2000	24.04	23.41	0.62 (0.19)	45.11	15.06	30.04[a] (6.18)

[a] Indicates statistically significance at the 1 per cent level.
Source: Fondazione Eni Enrico Mattei.

We now beg a final question. Is it possible to identify economic reasons to rationalize governments' reluctance to sell, or has it to be traced back to their willingness to keep companies under political control? More precisely, are there idiosyncratic factors—maybe related to a given country, sector, or business activity—which could explain why some SOEs are so tightly controlled?

One possible way of testing this hypothesis is to construct a control sample of private firms, and then to compare the evolution of the ultimate ownership within the two samples.

In order to find matching firms for privatized companies, some methodological issues have to be addressed. First, one has to establish objective criteria to compare firms, and then identify the rules for sampling. Ideally, the matching firm should operate in the same country, in the same sector, and be of comparable size. In some cases, it is not possible to find a private firm matching these stringent criteria and slightly different rules for sampling have to be adopted.[5] However, the majority of companies fits in the first best case.

Table 5.3 reports some statistics on the ultimate ownership of privatized companies as opposed to their respective matching private firms. The pooled data suggest a strong convergence between the privatized firms and the control sample. The samples report a statistically significant difference in means of approximately 8 per cent in 1996, which becomes insignificant and negligible in 2000.

Therefore—on average—privatized companies tend to look like their private counterparts in the long run. This evidence is consistent with the results obtained when analysing the dynamics of ownership in privatized firms. Indeed, we have discovered that about three-quarters of our companies in 2000 are widely held corporations, or owned by large private shareholders. But what is the evolution of ownership in 'state-owned' companies as

---

[5] The rules for sampling are described in detail in Appendix 1, Data and Methodology.

opposed to their matching firms? In this sub-sample, ownership structures do not converge at all. On average, the public shareholder owns a stake which is 30 per cent larger than the one owned by the largest ultimate private shareholder. The magnitude and statistical significance of this difference persists at the end of the period.

This evidence about the dynamics of ownership in privatized companies allows a deeper understanding of governments' reluctance to sell. On average, the privatization process has contributed to the roll-back of the state in the ownership of productive assets. Several companies have been sold off, and in these companies the governments do not appear as the major shareholders post-privatization. However, there is also a hard core of companies which remains tightly controlled by the state over time. Partial privatization appears to be a stable outcome for this subset of firms.

5.4. GOLDEN SHARES AND SPECIAL RIGHTS

The previous analyses allow us to draw a first conclusion. In developed economies, the transfer of ownership rights from the state to the private sector has been significant, but systematically incomplete. As already mentioned, in the majority of countries, the state is still the largest shareholder in several firms.

Indeed, many state-owned enterprises were fully privatized during the 1990s. However, the sale of a majority holding is not itself a sufficient condition to avoid government interference in privatized companies. Governments can grant themselves wide discretionary powers over partially or even fully privatized companies by the use of 'golden shares'. By exerting its rights, the 'special' shareholder can often influence the choice of management, exert veto power over the acquisition of relevant stakes by private shareholders, even without owning the majority of stock in the company, or a single share of capital.

The main consequence of golden shares is the separation of property rights from control rights. Starting from Berle and Means (1932) seminal contribution, the corporate finance literature has clarified the agency problem stemming from this separation (Jensen and Meckling 1976; Grossman and Hart 1980). When it occurs, controlling shareholders may abuse their power to expropriate outside investors. The financial incentives to reap private benefits of control are obviously moderated by equity of cash flow ownership, which should also enhance corporate valuation.

The separation of ownership and control induced by golden share mechanisms may be costly for privatizing governments, as it will be discounted in privatization prices. If so, why are golden shares so widely used?

A possible reason could be found in the politicians' willingness to interfere in the operating activity of privatized firms (Shleifer and Vishny 1994). The opportunity cost in terms of lower revenue then has to be compared with the benefit of ongoing political control.

However, at the first stage of the privatization process, golden shares may serve the public purpose of defending national interests in strategic sectors (i.e. energy, utilities, aerospace, national airlines, etc.), by providing a shield against hostile take-overs by unwelcome investors, and giving the newly privatized firms a limited time to adjust to the market.[6]

This was the rationale for the special shares in the United Kingdom. The British government took stock of the experience of the privatization of British Petroleum, the national oil monopoly and Britain's largest company by far.

BP was privatized without any golden share through a series of issues from 1977 to October 1987, when the government came to sell its remaining 31.5 per cent shareholding. By early 1988, the Kuwait Investment Office (KIO) began building up a stake in BP which in a few months amounted to 21.7 per cent of the company's share capital. The possibility that a foreign public shareholder might control the company raised alarms in the English establishment, and in political debate, and also because huge BP assets in Kuwait were nationalized.

After an investigation by the UK's Monopolies and Mergers Commission, the government endorsed the Commission's findings that the KIO's holding could operate against the public interest. The KIO was therefore required to reduce its stake to not more than 9.9 per cent of BP's stock. In 1989, BP purchased (and then cancelled) 790 million BP shares from the KIO, at three times the issue price.

While it is certainly difficult to rationalize golden shares on efficiency grounds, in some cases national industrial policy objectives could be set forth to support them. In others, the notion of protecting the public interest is little more than an alibi for maintaining public control and raising legal barriers around the country's most important companies.

In this section, we investigate these matters, and try to answer to the following questions. Are golden shares widespread around the world? In which sectors are they more widely used? Does the extent of special powers vary across countries? Is their use and intensity somehow related to the extent of privatization?

In our research on golden shares mechanisms around the world, we start by a definition.

We define the 'Golden Share' as the complex of special powers granted to the state, and the statutory constraints on privatized companies. Typically, special powers include (i) the right to appoint members on the corporate board; (ii) the right to express a consent or to veto the acquisition of relevant interests in the privatized companies; (iii) other rights such as consent on the transfer of subsidiaries, dissolution of the company, ordinary management, etc. The above mentioned rights may be temporary or not. Statutory constraints include (i) ownership limits; (ii) voting caps; (iii) provisions of national control.

---

[6] Paradoxically, by defining clearly the powers held by government or its representatives, it may allow private investors to assess better the effective value of shares on sale.

This set of powers and constraints may stem from the possession of a redeemable special share, from limitations imposed by the privatized company's statutes, often in accordance with the privatization law, and from the possession of special class shares.

Starting from this broad definition, we can now carry out a cross country analysis on the application of golden shares in privatized companies.[7] However, listed companies are forced to disclose fully the presence of golden shares mechanisms in their prospectuses. We have therefore solicited privatization prospectuses from individual companies, investment banks, security exchange commissions, and privatization agencies. We have been able to obtain 104 prospectuses from our sample of 143 companies privatized in OECD countries in the 1977–2000 period.[8]

We have then singled out in the company's prospectus the presence of golden shares. At first approximation, a privatized company is labelled *cum* golden share if its prospectus features *at least one* of the special powers or constraints listed above. Albeit rough, this information allows us to verify whether the use of golden shares is common, or confined to a bunch of protectionist countries.

This preliminary analysis enables us to provide two important answers. In developed economies, golden shares mechanisms are indeed widespread, and typically concentrated in strategic sectors. First, golden shares are found in more than 50 per cent of the companies in our sample, and in each and everyone of the twenty-two countries with the exceptions of Finland and the US.[9] Second, they are highly concentrated in some sectors, such as defence, where 100 per cent of the privatized companies have golden shares, telecommunications (83 per cent), oil and gas (62 per cent), utility (64 per cent) and transports (40 per cent). Special powers and statutory constraints are instead quite absent in agricultural, industrial, manufacturing, and banking sectors, appearing only in 28 per cent of the companies.

Not surprisingly, the data show clearly that governments resort to golden shares in order to protect a broadly defined concept of 'national security'. Indeed, this objective can easily be traced back in the shielding of privatized companies in the defence business from hostile (foreign) take-overs. However, it may also apply in the protection of utilities providing public services, such as gas, electricity, water, telecommunications, and transports. The provision of such services but also the

---

[7] Detailed institutional information about golden shares can be found from some official web sites (such as the HM Treasury in the United Kingdom, *www.hm-treasury.gov.uk*, the Spanish Sociedad Estatal de Participaciones Industriales, *www.sepi.es*, the Austrian Holding and Privatization Agency, *www.oiag.at*).

[8] The information refers only to companies privatized by SIP and sold by the central governments. Companies privatized by asset sales, sold by regional governments or administrative bodies, spin-offs from state-controlled corporations, and companies still fully owned by the state are excluded.

[9] Interestingly, the United States operates a similar system via the Exon-Florio Amendment (1988) which gives the Committee on Foreign Investment in the United States (CFIUS) the power to block take-overs of any American company if it is seen to pose a threat to national security. However, they do not apply in the privatization context, so it has been excluded from the analysis.

safeguard of essential facilities are certainly strategic, especially when privatization did not proceed in parallel with adequate liberalization and effective regulation. In these circumstances, golden shares could provide a partial substitute.

The focus on strategic sectors is the key to a full understanding of the use of golden shares. In what follows, we will investigate the issue, carrying out a more detailed analysis for a subset of firms operating in those critical sectors.

5.5. MEASURING GOLDEN SHARES IN STRATEGIC SECTORS

In Appendix 3, Table A3.1 shows the complete list of companies privatized in OECD economies operating in strategic sectors. A sector is considered strategic if a broad national interest could be identified in the operating activity of its companies. The following sectors fall into this category: aerospace and defence, oil and gas, electricity, telecommunications, and transports. The table singles out the companies privatized with and without golden shares, along with the government residual stake as of 2002.

Clearly, our classification of companies with golden shares is unsatisfactory as it does not take into account the extent of the special powers of the state and of the limits imposed on private shareholders. As we can see in Appendix 3, the content of golden shares varies greatly across countries and companies. In some cases, governments' extraordinary powers are combined with substantial constraints so that golden shares become an extremely powerful instrument to control privatized companies. In other cases, the state's discretionary powers are more limited.

Table 5.4 provides a finer analysis by introducing our indicator of the scope or 'intensity' of the golden share in privatized companies operating in strategic sectors. The measure is based on the classification used to define golden shares and is simply given by the number of special powers and statutory constraints found in the company prospectuses. The measure is constructed under the assumption that a higher number of these components is associated with a more restrictive golden share.

This indicator suffers from some limitations. First, it relies on a rather general classification, disregarding important institutional details. For example, the generic label 'power to appoint members of the board of directors' does not weigh this power by the effective number of directors the governments can appoint (see Appendix 3). When considering ownership limits or voting caps, we do not take into account the different thresholds imposed (see Appendix 3). Second, in the construction of the indicator every component is given an equal weight. Despite its limits, our measure allows a consistent comparison across companies and countries by limiting researchers' discretion.

A first look at Table 5.4 shows that the intensity of the golden share varies substantially across companies. Our variable yields the top value (5) in Finmeccanica (the Italian defence company), in British Energy (English electricity generation companies with nuclear facilities), and Portugal Telecom,

Table 5.4. *Intensity of the golden shares (as of 2002)*

Country	Company	Powers to appoint BoD (1)	Powers to veto M&A	Other veto powers (2)	Ownership limits	Voting caps	National control (3)	Intensity	Country average intensity
Italy	Eni	x	x		x	x		4	4.3
	Enel	x	x		x	x		4	
	Telecom Italia	x	x		x	x		4	
	Finmeccanica	x	x	x	x	x		5	
UK	British Energy	x	x	x	x		x	5	2.6
	Scottish Power		x		x			2	
	Scottish & Southern Energy		x		x			2	
	National Grid Group		x		x			2	
	Viridian Group		x		x			2	
	Rolls Royce		x	x	x			3	
	British Aerospace		x	x	x			3	
	Baa plc		x	x	x			3	
	Railtrack Group		x					1	
France	Totalfina Elf	x	x	x				3	3.5
	Thales	x	x	x	x			4	
Spain	Repsol Ypf		x		x			2	1.4
	Endesa		x					1	
	Telefonica		x					1	
	Indra Systemas		x	x				2	
	Iberia		x					1	

Country	Company						No.[1]	%[3]
Portugal	Electricitade de Portugal	x	x		x		2	3.0
	Portugal Telecom	x	x		x		5	
Austria	Verbund	x	x		x		3	3.0
Denmark	TeleDanmark			x	x		1	1.0
	Copenhagen Airports			x	x		1	
Netherlands	KPN	x	x		x		2	2.0
	KLM Airlines	x			x	x	2	
	TNT PG		x		x		2	
Belgium	Distrigaz	x	x		x		4	4.0
Greece	Hellenic Petroleum		x	x	x		3	3.0
	Ote		x	x	x		3	
Australia	Telestra Corp.				x		1	2.0
	Qantas Airways		x		x	x	3	
Canada	PetroCanada	x	x		x	x	3	2.8
	Alberta Energy		x		x		1	
	Nova Scotia P.H.			x	x		3	
	Telus Corp.	x	x		x	x	4	
	Air Canada			x	x	x	3	
Japan	NTT			x	x		1	1.0
New Zealand	Telecom Corp		x	x	x		3	3.0
	Air New Zealand			x	x		3	

(1) The power to appoint may refer to one or more members of the Board of Directors (BoD), and/or the Chairman.

(2) It can include the veto on acquisitions of subsidiaries.

(3) National control is referred to the case when the company statute prohibits non-residents to acquire a controlling interest in the privatized company. The provision in EU regulation (2407/92) for air transport sector (requiring that air carriers must be owned and effectively controlled by Member States or nationals of Member States to be entitled to benefit from the Third Liberalization Package measures) is *not* included.

Source: Fondazione Eni Enrico Mattei.

the former Portuguese national telecommunication monopoly. The lowest value of our index (1) appears in Railtrack (the company was placed in liquidation and de-listed in 2002), in some Spanish companies (such as Endesa, Telefonica, and Iberia), in all Danish companies, Telstra (an Australian telecommunication operator) and in Alberta Energy (a Canadian electric utility).

The data collected allow us to investigate in detail the use and intensity of the golden share in companies privatized in strategic sectors of OECD countries. However, a comprehensive analysis of golden shares must be carried out jointly with the study of government residual stakes. Indeed, golden shares exhibit strategic value in fully or almost fully privatized companies, where governments' direct stakes do not allow for the exercise of control.

Table 5.5 presents the data at the country level. With the exception of the United Kingdom, Australia, and Spain, the government is still a large shareholder in companies operating in strategic sectors, with an average stake of more than 32 per cent. Interestingly, despite the relatively large stake, the governments also often hold golden shares. On average, they appear in more than half of companies privatized in those sectors.

Indeed, golden shares are widely used. However, several companies operating in strategic sectors do *not* have any golden shares. This information is interesting and shows that these sectors are not 'strategic' *per se*, but they probably become strategic and as such warrant special protection when they are more fully privatized.

Figure 5.1 partly confirms this intuition. If we plot the country averages of the stakes sold against the percentage of firms with golden shares, the slope of the regression line indicates that the frequency of golden shares is higher in countries closer to full privatization.

Table 5.5 provides a cross country comparison of the intensity of the golden share. Interestingly, our measure displays a large variability across OECD economies. Some continental European countries such as Italy, Belgium,

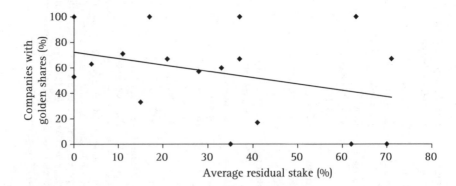

Figure 5.1. *Average residual stake and companies with golden shares at a country level*

Table 5.5. *Residual average stake and golden shares*

Country	Privatized companies	Average residual stake (%)	Companies with golden shares (%)	Average residual stake in companies with golden shares (%)	Intensity of the golden shares
Australia	2	0	100	0	2.0
Austria	6	41	17	51	3.0
Belgium	1	17	100	17	4.0
Canada	7	11	71	3.7	2.8
Denmark	2	63	100	63	1.0
Finland	1	62	0	–	–
France	4	33	60	16	3.5
Germany	3	35	0	–	–
Greece	3	71	67	71	3.0
Italy	7	28	57	33	4.3
Japan	3	15	33	46	1.0
Netherlands	3	37	100	37	2.0
New Zealand	3	21	67	0	2.0
Norway	3	70	0	–	–
Portugal	3	37	67	18	3.5
Spain	8	4	63	0	1.4
UK	17	0	53	0	2.6
Average	4.5	32	56	25.2	2.0

Sector	Privatized companies	Average residual stake (%)	Average residual stake (UK excluded) (%)	Companies with golden shares (%)	Companies with golden shares (UK excluded) (%)	Average residual stake in companies with golden shares (%)	Average residual stake in companies with golden shares (UK excluded) (%)	Intensity of the golden shares	Intensity of the golden shares (UK excluded)
Oil and gas	15	27.72	31.98	47	54	20.31	20.32	2.9	2.9
Electricity	18	14.08	25.24	55	50	14.92	29.88	2.6	2.6
Tlc	16	26.94	30.76	62	71	20.17	20.17	2.5	2.5
Aerospace and defence	6	19.23	28.83	83	75	13.01	21.68	3.4	3.7
Transport	21	24.96	29.13	38	39	16.74	21.53	2.1	2.0

Source: Fondazione Eni Enrico Mattei.

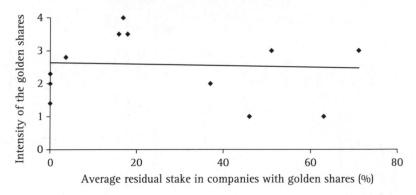

Figure 5.2. *Average residual stake in companies with golden shares and its intensity at a country level*

Source: Fondazione Eni Enrico Mattei.

Portugal, and France provide governments with a powerful instrument to protect strategic interests, with values for the intensity of the golden shares well above the average. However, a more powerful golden share is not at all associated with more complete privatization. As Figure 5.2 shows, the flat regression line does not suggest any relation between the residual stakes and the intensity of the golden share.

Why are some countries so eager to keep privatized companies under state control? Why do others privatize fully without granting governments residual powers or limiting shareholders' rights?

A possible answer can be given by the different sectors involved in privatization. Some companies may be considered truly strategic as they provide public goods which are essential for national security. Other companies may or may not become strategic in relation to the extent of privatization and liberalization of the respective sector of activity. In other words, privatized monopolies (especially in network industries and utilities) are more likely to be considered 'strategic', and as such need a more extensive protection through golden shares.

The analysis of the data at the sector level confirms that these factors play some role. As Table 5.5 shows, the highest frequency of golden shares is found in the aerospace and defence, certainly a key sector for national security, which has also been quite extensively privatized. Interestingly, it also displays the highest absolute value for the intensity of the golden shares, confirming the strategic role of the sector. The data point out a negative relationship between the extent of privatization and the use of golden shares, which is partly in line with what emerged at the country level. Finally, it is also interesting to note that less restrictive (and therefore less powerful) golden shares are found in more heavily liberalized sectors such as telecommunications and electricity.

5.6. CONCLUSIONS

Our empirical analysis shows that governments are often reluctant to lose control of privatized firms, and this reluctance appears particularly strong in the so-called strategic sectors. This defensive attitude can certainly be attributed to governments' willingness to maintain firm political control over their country's largest and most valuable corporations (often defined as the 'crown jewels'). However, the failure to relinquish control has also to be traced back to the various economic and institutional constraints shaping economic policy. Indeed, genuine privatization is problematic if markets are not competitive, and regulation is weak.

Exactly for these reasons, even if exogenous conditions would allow for the resumption of the privatization process, it is likely that the coexistence of private ownership with public control could represent a stable outcome.

6

Privatizing Monopolies

6.1. INTRODUCTION

On a worldwide scale, privatization appears to follow a common pattern. In virtually all major regions, however, including Western Europe, Latin America, Oceania, the former Soviet Union, the Middle East, North Africa, and Asia, the percentage of revenue from the sale of utilities appears to be increasing over time (see Figures 6.1 to 6.9).

Despite this common trend, privatization processes evolve at different speeds. As we have seen in the previous chapter, only a few countries have fully privatized strategic sectors such as energy, telecommunications, or transport. The UK went furthest in privatization in the shortest time. The Thatcher government started in 1977 with British Petroleum (BP), the national oil company, followed by companies of the industry sector. By the end of the 1980s, the process experienced an abrupt acceleration, with privatization of water and sewerage, electricity, TLC and, more recently, railways. Similarly, Argentina has rapidly entered the more advanced stage. The privatization process started in 1990 with important sales in utilities. From 1990 to 1996, 88 per cent of sales occurred in strategic sectors, mainly in the electricity and gas distribution sector.

Some ambitious privatization programmes experienced an abrupt interruption despite a promising start. For instance, as we have seen in Chapter 2, Section 2.3, French privatization started in 1986–87 in the financial and banking sector. The first sale in the energy sector took place in 1992 with the partial sale of Elf Aquitaine and Total. After a long interruption, the process regained momentum in 1997 with the sale of France Telecom. Notwithstanding some recent announcements, the majority of assets in strategic sectors are still publicly owned.

The Italian experience is similar. The privatization process started in 1985 with partial sales of SIRTI and Alitalia. From 1985 to 1995, sales involved mainly the industry and banking sectors. The first large flotation in the utility sector took place a decade after the start of privatization, with the first divested piece of Eni, the national oil company. Since then, some significant sales have occurred in the utilities (Eni and Telecom Italia). However, the privatization of electricity has been only partial, and the privatization of railways is still wishful thinking.

In this chapter, we argue that regulation is the key to the divestiture of monopolies. The privatization process can then smoothly enter the second stage involving utilities only if governments have injected competition into the market and structured a clear regulatory framework before privatization. A well-defined

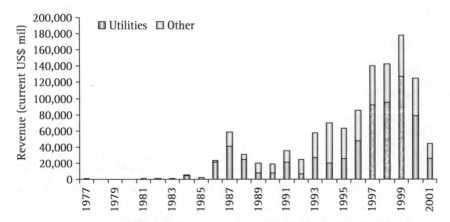

Figure 6.1. *Distribution of revenue by sector around the world (1977–2001)**

*Detailed definitions of geographical regions can be found in Chapter 2. For the definition of *Utilities* see also Chapter 2; *Other* include all industrial sectors that do not belong to Utilities.

Source: Elaboration on *Privatisation International*, and *Securities Data Corporation*.

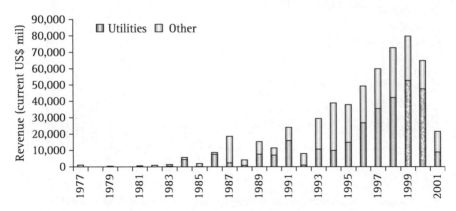

Figure 6.2. *Distribution of revenue by sector in Western Europe (1977–2001)**

*Detailed definitions of geographical regions can be found in Chapter 2. For the definition of *Utilities* see also Chapter 2; *Other* include all industrial sectors that do not belong to Utilities.

Source: Elaboration on *Privatisation International*, and *Securities Data Corporation*.

regulatory framework is crucial in privatization since it provides a substitute for public ownership, avoiding the pitfalls of private ownership of natural monopolies. It should allow governments to sell more companies in the utility sector and, more importantly, to transfer the ownership rights in the private sector, reducing the risks of expropriation (Spiller 1995).

Regulation may also determine the success of privatization in terms of proceeds. Conventional wisdom suggests that regulation decreases the expected profitability of the investment, given that post-privatization firms will be more heavily constrained in their pricing decisions (Vickers and Yarrow 1988). Given rational

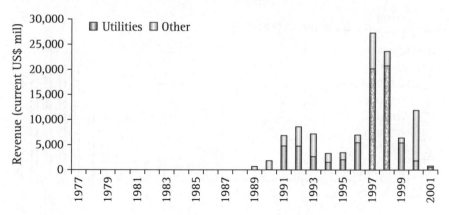

Figure 6.3. *Distribution of revenue by sector in Latin America (1977–2001)**
* See note to Figure 6.2.
Source: Elaboration on *Privatisation International*, and *Securities Data Corporation*.

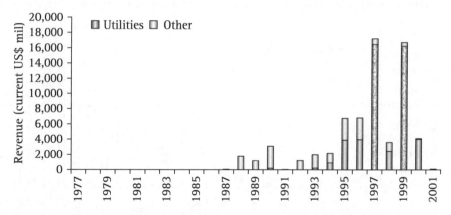

Figure 6.4. *Distribution of revenue by sector in Oceania (1977–2001)**
* See note to Figure 6.2.
Source: Elaboration on *Privatisation International*, and *Securities Data Corporation*.

expectations by investors, future profitability will be perfectly anticipated at the time of the sale. Governments may therefore face a trade-off between revenue maximization and allocative efficiency. On the other hand, regulatory risk also affects value. In the absence of regulation, the contract struck by investors and a government privatizing a utility will be particularly incomplete. It is prohibitively costly to specify *ex ante* all possible actions that should be taken if the government decides to renegotiate the previous agreement and regulate the market *ex post*. Contract incompleteness typically generates under-investment in specific assets, which will be reflected in the price agreed upon in the initial contract. A clear regulatory setting can reduce transaction costs and generate a

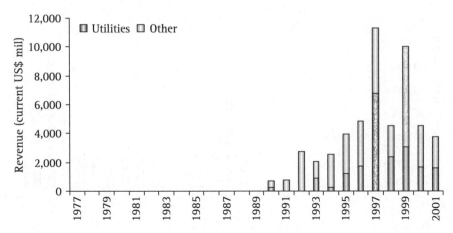

Figure 6.5. *Distribution of revenue by sector in the CEECs and the former Soviet Union (1977–2001)**

* See note to Figure 6.2.

Source: Elaboration on *Privatisation International*, and *Securities Data Corporation*.

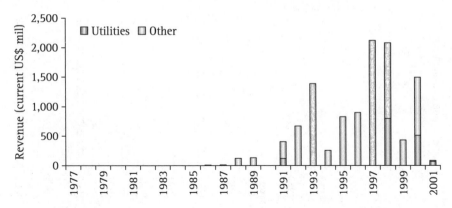

Figure 6.6. *Distribution of revenue by sector in Mena (1977–2001)**

* See note to Figure 6.2.

Source: Elaboration on *Privatisation International*, and *Securities Data Corporation*.

premium on privatization proceeds (Williamson 1985; Hart and Moore 1988; Klein *et al.* 1978).

Regulation is not the only factor explaining the pace of divestiture in network industries. An additional factor is the market structure, as privatization may prove particularly difficult in vertically integrated systems. Selling a vertically integrated business is not efficient, since cross-subsidies are possible. As demonstrated by the BP and British Gas experience, when governments attempt to increase the competitiveness of the market after privatization, the integrated

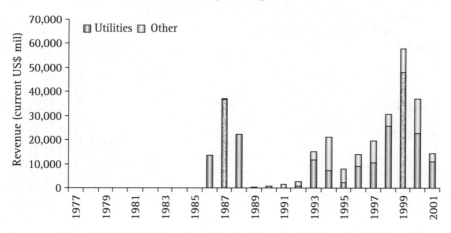

Figure 6.7. *Distribution of revenue by sector in Asia (1977–2001)**

*See note to Figure 6.2.

Source: Elaboration on *Privatisation International*, and *Securities Data Corporation*.

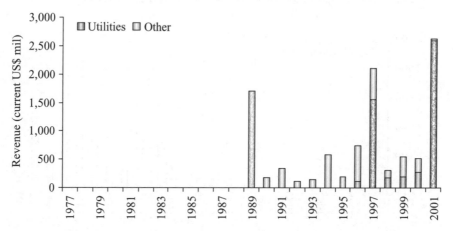

Figure 6.8. *Distribution of revenue by sector in sub-Saharan Africa (1977–2001)**

*See note to Figure 6.2.

Source: Elaboration on *Privatisation International*, and *Securities Data Corporation*.

incumbent is typically able to subsidize the competitive side of the business and stifle entry (Helm and Jenkinson 1998). These concerns lead benevolent governments and regulators to recommend unbundling of the activities before privatization. Unbundling and liberalization is difficult, however, where a powerful player dominates the market, since it can exert pressure at the legislative stage to maintain the *status quo*.

The objective of this chapter is to assess the effect of market structure and regulation on privatization. We address this issue by carrying out a cross country

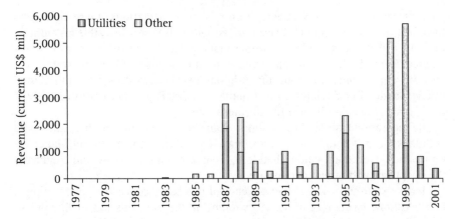

Figure 6.9. *Distribution of revenue by sector in North America and the Caribbean (1977–2001)**

* See note to Figure 6.2.

Source: Elaboration on *Privatisation International*, and *Securities Data Corporation*.

empirical analysis in one of the most relevant privatized sectors, electricity. But before starting these systematic analyses, we report the case of Argentina, which shows how regulation could be the key in the success or failure of the privatization of monopolies.

6.2. PRIVATIZATION, RIGHT AND WRONG: THE CASE OF ARGENTINE UTILITIES

In 1989, the newly elected peronist President Menem launched an ambitious privatization programme, starting with the sale of Entel, the national telecommunications operator.

The sale turned out to be particularly difficult, due especially to regulatory uncertainty. Even before privatization, because of strong internal pressures, attempts to liberalize and regulate the sector came asunder. Indeed, the government, initially wanting to fully unbundle Entel into five companies, created only two regional groups (Entel North and Entel South). Further, the regulatory authority was not yet functional at the time of privatization even though it had been established by law in April of 1990 (Manzetti 1997).

The economic prospects of the business are extremely interesting but the institutional context is not transparent, especially due to well-grounded suspicions of corruption.

The government sensed investor feeling and chose to intervene through a number of decrees aimed at increasing the value of the investment. Hence, the following incentives were introduced: (i) an extension of five to seven years on licenses for urban and long-distance calls, with the option of further prolongation pending certain investments; (ii) a substantial upward revision of the guaranteed return on investment. Contrary to expectations, these incentives have had the opposite effect. Instead of assuaging investor fear, this last-minute fiddling with the terms of the contract made palpable the risk of *ex post* interference from the government, perhaps in the opposite direction. When the auction began, only three of the original twelve investors who manifested interest made offers: Telefonica de Espana won Entel's southern division and the Stet-France Telecom alliance the northern one.

The operation raised $1.2 billion. Plausibly, some of the investors who withdrew shortly before the auction may have been prepared to bid higher for Entel. The government could, therefore, have raised more money and conducted the operation with greater transparency.

Finally, a further negative consequence of this badly conceived privatization is that telephone tariffs rose in the years following the sale. This was mainly due to the lack of competition on the market and the weakness of regulation (Figure 6.10).

This negative experience was important for learning how not to privatize. Indeed, the subsequent sale of the electricity sector is planned very carefully, keeping the objectives of liberalization and regulation firmly in focus through all of its phases. Firstly, the government gives immediate operational power to an independent regulatory authority. Secondly, it carries out a profound restructuring of the market, with both vertical and horizontal de-integration, creating twenty-one different generation companies, three big distributors and one new company. Thirdly, it establishes a wholesale electricity market (pool) to stimulate competition between generators and distributors, simultaneously permitting bilateral contracts between big users.

The privatization of Argentina's electricity sector is still considered exemplary, managing, as it did, to attract a large number of investors and, as a consequence, generating considerable revenue compared with similar operations

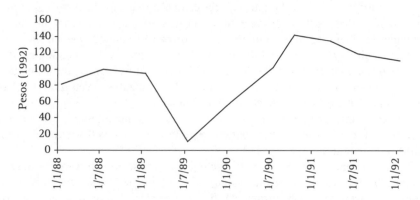

Figure 6.10. *Entel prices (1988–1992)*

Source: Petrazzini 1996.

in the same sector. Given the competition in the market, electricity tariffs fell substantially after privatization, with savings of up to 40 per cent for Argentina's consumers compared with the preceding period (Manzetti 1997).

Naturally, we are not allowed to draw general conclusions from a single example. More convincing results may, however, emerge from the empirical analysis described in the following sections.

6.3. PRIVATIZING ELECTRICITY

For the period 1977 to 2001, privatization in the energy sector (oil and gas and electricity) involved over 750 sales and $327 billion in revenue around the world (80 per cent of revenue in electricity and 20 per cent in oil and gas). We restrict our analysis to electricity for two main reasons: first, sales account for the largest proportion of the revenue; second, oil and gas includes regulated as well as unregulated segments of the sector. This analysis is further restricted to sales in power generation, excluding transmission and distribution mainly because more countries have been involved in privatization of the upstream segment of the industry. It considers companies involved in generation alone, and excludes partially integrated operators, such as distributors with some generation capacity or generators that own segments of the transmission network. Sales are listed in Table 6.1.

The choice of the sample is mainly determined by the availability of reliable data about the electricity industry and regulation. We started with the forty-nine country samples used in this book (see Chapter 3). From that sample, regulatory and market structure indicators were retrieved for thirty-eight countries, mainly drawn from Lewington (1997), a leading source for institutional and legal materials concerning regulated sectors. For the countries not included in that source, original national documents were relied upon.[1]

The analysis at the company level is based upon data for forty-eight generators in nineteen countries.[2]

From these data, we have constructed the following privatization variables: (i) the total number of sales in electricity generation in a given country (*ELSALES*); (ii) the per country aggregate proceeds from total sales in 1996 US$ (*ELREVENUES*); (iii) the stake privatized at the firm level (*ELSTOCK*), taking into account multiple issues, if any.

---

[1] The UK has been desegregated into England and Wales, Scotland and Northern Ireland, mainly because market structure differs substantially in the three regions. England and Wales are separate systems, with a high degree of competition in generation, given the existence of a wholesale electricity market (the 'pool'). In contrast, in Scotland, there are two vertically integrated operators (Scottish Power and Scottish Hydro). In Northern Ireland, a single company operates in both transmission and distribution (Northern Ireland Electricity), but three generators are present. Furthermore, a separate regulator (Ofreg) has responsibility for both gas and electricity.

[2] The description of the variables appears in Appendix 1, Data and Methodology.

Table 6.1. *Privatization in electricity generation (1977–1997)*

Country	Company	Date	Type	ElRevenue (US$ billion)	ElStock
Argentina	Segba (Puerto)	01/03/92	Private sale	0.09	60
	Segba (Costanera)	01/05/92		0.09	60
	Alto Valle	01/09/92	Private sale	0.02	90
	Dock Sud	01/09/92	Private Sale	0.03	90
	Guemes	01/09/92	Private sale	0.09	60
	Segba(Pedro de Mendoza)	01/09/92	Private sale	0.01	90
	Alicura	01/07/93		0.39	59
	Cerros Colorado	01/07/93		0.18	59
	El Chocon	01/07/93		0.53	59
	Hidroelectrica Piedra del Aguila (Hidronor)	01/12/93	Private sale	0.27	59
	Ameghino	01/06/94		0.02	59
	Futaleufu	01/04/95	Private sale	0.23	98
	Dirrecion Provincial de Energia	10/07/96	Private sale	0.05	60
	Luis Piedrabuena de Bahia Blanca plant (Eseba)	31/07/97	Private sale	0.03	100
Australia	Loy Yang B power station	01/01/93	Private sale	1.01	40
	Yallourn Energy	05/03/96	Private sale	1.88	100
	Hazelwood	01/08/96	Private sale	1.83	100
	Loy Yang B	01/04/97	Private sale	0.78	49
	Loy Yang A	22/04/97	Private sale	3.80	100
	Southern Hydro	21/11/97	Private sale	0.27	100
Austria	Verbund (Oesterreichische Elektrizitaetswirtschaft)	01/11/88	Public offer	0.44	49
	EVN Energie-Versorgung Niederosterreich	17/11/89	Public offer	0.13	25
Brazil	COPEL	17/01/97	Public offer	0.09	8.27

Table **6.1.** (*Cont.*)

Country	Company	Date	Type	ElRevenue (US$ billion)	ElStock
	Cachoeira Dourada			0.71	100
Canada	Nova Scotia Power	12/08/92	Public Offer	0.68	100
Chile	Colbun- Machicura	01/01/96		0.41	44.2
	Tocopilla	01/11/96	Private Sale	0.18	51
Colombia	499 MW Betania hydroelectric plant	19/12/96	Private Sale	0.30	99
	1,000 MW Chivor hydroelectric plant	20/12/96	Private Sale	0.64	100
England and Wales	National Power (Gencos 1)	06/03/91	Public Offer	1.40	60
	PowerGen (Gencos 1)	06/03/91	Public Offer	2.28	60
	National Power (Gencos 2)	01/03/95	Public Offer	2.81	40
	PowerGen Gencos 2)	01/03/95	Public Offer	1.87	40
	British Energy	10/07/96	Public Offer	2.18	87.73
Finland	Kemijoki Oy	01/02/97		0.43	25
Germany	Rhein-Main-Donau (RMD)	05/07/94	Private Sale	0.45	75.5
	Neckar	31/12/95	Private Sale	0.10	99
Northern Ireland	Ballylumford power station (Northern Ireland Electricity)	01/04/92	Private Sale	0.22	100
	Coolkeeragh power station (Northern Ireland Electricity)	01/04/92	Private Sale	0.01	100
	Kilroot, Belfast West power stations (Northern Ireland Electricity)	01/04/92	Private Sale	0.35	100
New Zealand	Mangahao Hydro Power Station	30/11/97	Private Sale	0.03	100
Pakistan	Kot Addu power station	03/04/96	Private Sale	0.22	26

Table 6.1. (*Cont.*)

Country	Company	Date	Type	ElRevenue (US$ billion)	ElStock
Peru	Cahua	25/04/95	Private Sale	0.04	60
	Edegel	17/10/95	Private Sale	0.52	60
	Ventanilla	12/12/95	Private Sale	0.12	60
Portugal	Pego Power	28/11/93	Private Sale	1.16	90
Scotland	Scottish Hydro Electric	12/06/91	Public Offer	1.72	100
	Scottish Power	12/06/91	Public Offer	3.67	100
Spain	Empresa Nacional de Eletricidad (ENDESA)	26/05/94		1.05	6.7
	ENDESA	21/10/97		4.56	25
United States	Milwaukee County power plant	01/12/94	Private Sale	0.06	100
Thailand	Electricity Generating Public Company (EGCO)	09/11/94		0.18	49

Source: Fondazione Eni Enrico Mattei.

6.4. VERTICAL INTEGRATION

The structure of the electricity sector varies greatly around the world, ranging from high concentration and vertical integration to more competitive and separated regimes. At one end of the spectrum, electricity is mainly provided by a single vertically integrated company operating nationwide. Many European countries fit this model: ENEL in Italy, EdF in France, the Electricity Supply Board in Ireland and PPC in Greece all operate in generation, transmission, and distribution under state control. In the Belgian and Austrian systems, different companies appear to be involved in different market segments, but a closer look at the ownership structures reveals a high degree of concentration of activities within a single entity. In Belgium, until October 1996, Tractebel owned a majority stake in Powerfin and a solid controlling position in Electrabel, which in turn owned the majority of stock in the 'mixed' inter-municipal companies that provide nearly 80 per cent of electricity distribution. In Austria, several companies are responsible for generation, transmission, and distribution.

Nevertheless, VG, the interstate interconnection transmission company, owns a majority stake upstream in eight generators and downstream through direct or indirect holdings in the several regional or municipal distribution companies. In both cases, vertical integration is completely replicated by ownership.

In other countries, there is less horizontal concentration of activities within a single firm or through shareholdings. However, a number of vertically integrated players often operates on a regional scale. For instance, Germany is horizontally decentralized, but the generation and transmission (and to some degree distribution) activities are regionally integrated in nine main utilities. A similar structure is also found in Denmark and Scotland, where supply consists of two vertically integrated regional systems.

At the other extreme of the spectrum are vertically separated and often more competitive settings. Vertical separation and liberalization are often the outcome of a process of deep restructuring of the industry via unbundling. These liberalization processes are particularly important for the scope of the present analysis, as they form a part of a well-designed privatization package.

England and Wales represent a blueprint for liberalization and restructuring in the electricity sector. Since the reform set forth in the 1988 White Paper was strictly implemented, the market has experienced horizontal and vertical separation. The Central Electricity Generating Board (CEGB) has been broken up into two generators (National Power and PowerGen), and the National Grid company. The Regional Electricity Boards were privatized as the Regional Electricity Companies (RECs) with responsibilities for the distribution and supply businesses (Green and Newbery 1998).

Some countries have followed the British model. In the early 1990s, Argentina experienced 'one of the most drastic, comprehensive and rapid sets of changes ever observed in the electricity services in a modern democracy' (Bastos and Abdala 1996). Until 1992, the electricity industry was publicly owned and mainly consisted of three vertically integrated operators (SEGBA, AyE, and Hidronor). The 1992 privatization law required competition and market mechanisms to be introduced and promoted whenever possible, which involved unbundling of activities. The recommendations of the law have been implemented through a split of the three companies into twenty-one generation companies, three distribution companies, and through a merger of high-voltage transmission into a newly incorporated company, Transener.

Following its 1992 legislative reform, Peru has to some extent implemented a radical horizontal and vertical separation of electric industry. The generation activity of Electroperu and Electrolima was split into various entities, while the regional companies kept distribution as their sole activity. Similar processes also occurred in Chile, Australia, and Spain.

For present purposes, the existence of a vertically integrated system within a given country must be quantified. The relevant information concerning the industry structure is captured by the dummy *VINT*, taking the value one where the market is dominated by a single player, by various vertically integrated players or by a single entity owning controlling stakes in the upstream and downstream electricity business.

Vertical integration may hinder privatization. As stated above, the sale of a vertically integrated business may not be efficient, since cross subsidies are possible. It appears that to achieve efficiency, issue of the shares of the electric companies is required, separating out the natural monopoly side of the business. But this splitting is problematic when vertically integrated incumbents dominate the market. We therefore expect a negative correlation between the *VINT* dummy with our first quantity variable, *ELSALES*.

Vertical integration could also have a negative impact on aggregate proceeds. Indeed, market structure affects profitability, as investors anticipate that they will have to compete in the generation business with vertically integrated players. If the regulatory regime is limited, the network owner retains substantial market power, and can grant access at more favourable conditions to its own generators. The presence of a vertically integrated incumbent may therefore discourage entry, with negative consequences on proceeds. To test this conjecture, the *VINT* dummy is introduced in the *ELREVENUES* regressions.

6.5. MARKET REGULATION

Regulation is a key element in infrastructure privatization. A well-designed regulatory framework protects consumers from monopoly abuses and investors from arbitrary political action, and provides incentives for efficient operation and investment (Braeutigam 1989; Laffont and Tirole 1993). But how can the quality of regulation be measured? Is it possible to rank the intensity of regulation across jurisdictions using objective indicators? Comparative study of different institutional arrangements is intrinsically a difficult task, but with appropriate restrictions of the field, the experiment yields some useful results.

In the cross section of countries studied here, with very few exceptions (Ireland, Thailand, Philippines, Venezuela, Austria), the electricity market is typically subject to some form of public control. This means that at least a legal document involving the companies operating in the sector has been adopted and has been in place until January 1997. However, the mere existence of a law involving electricity provides little information; more details are needed on what has been regulated and the institutions designed to enforce the existing regulation.

The more interesting aspects of regulation in electricity generation and distribution involve: (i) entry conditions; (ii) access to the network; (iii) prices. The regulation of market access varies greatly around the world. In most countries, producers must meet certain requirements to obtain a licence, such as capacity, safety, environmental protection, etc. These requirements are often allocated on the basis of competitive bidding or other procedures.

While licences or the imposition of some standard upon generators are common features of entry regulations almost everywhere, countries differ systematically in the way the access to the network is regulated. The two sides of electricity supply—generation and local distribution—are linked through the network. For competition to be effective, access to natural monopoly bottlenecks should be guaranteed by law, and access rates suitably regulated. In some jurisdictions, network access is guaranteed to all producers and all eligible customers under objective and non-discriminatory conditions (regulated Third Party Access or TPA). In others, however, it is left to the benevolence of the network owner. An intermediate case is Negotiated TPA, under which generators have granted access to the network, but on conditions that depend on the agreement with distributors.

The TPA model is explicitly indicated in the European Directive for the Internal Electricity Market. Member States that have liberalized network access via regulated TPA include Denmark, Finland, Sweden, England and Wales, and the Netherlands. Negotiated TPA has been adopted in Austria, Portugal, and Germany.[3]

Another important institutional aspect of the functioning of the electricity market is the presence of a 'pool' or a regulated wholesale electricity market. The pool is an organized market for trading in electricity: generators compete to supply power to the grid. The existence of a pool is an element of regulation because, in most circumstances, it has been introduced by law and is a good indicator of the effectiveness of regulation in fuelling competition among generators.

A wholesale market for electricity was first established in Chile in the 1980s, in the United Kingdom in 1990, and in Argentina in 1992. Competitive pools are also operational in Scandinavia (the Nordpool, which has linked Norway and Sweden since 1992, and the EL-EX in Finland since 1996), in Spain since 1996, and in parts of the USA, Australia, and New Zealand.

Finally, the price formation mechanism is also regulated at various levels, typically in transmission and distribution. Excluding more exotic solutions, prices of the network owner are subject to RPI-X or rate of return regulation. Control of the price formation mechanism is crucial for the efficiency of the system. Virtually all countries that have a regulation concerning the electricity market somehow regulate prices. Since no proxy for the 'quality' of price regulation across countries is available (i.e. the X in RPI-X), it is excluded from this analysis.

Economists often neglect the institutional aspects of regulation.[4] Nevertheless, they warrant attention, since they provide valuable information as to how regulation is enforced. This analysis attempts to establish whether the law

---

[3] Regulation of grid access in Germany is enforced by the competition authority.

[4] Some recent contributions in economic analysis are taking the institutional aspect of regulation of the electricity market very seriously. Zhang, Parker, and Kirkpatrick (2002) provide an econometric assessment of the effects of privatization, competition, and regulation on the performance of the electricity generation industry in developing countries, showing that emphasis should be placed on implementing an effective regulatory framework. Wallsten (2001) adopts a similar approach.

in a given jurisdiction foresees an independent regulatory agency that is not merely advisory. Here, 'independent' means that the agency is not a branch of a ministry, and is engaged only in arm's length relationships with regulated firms and political authorities, facing low risks of being captured by firms or governments. 'Not advisory' means that the agency is endowed with decision-making powers to set and enforce tariffs, to establish regulations concerning security and quality standards, interruptions and reconnections, and metering and billing.

In most countries, a ministry (Energy, Industry, Development, etc.) is directly charged with regulatory functions. In some cases, a regulatory agency exists but is not independent of government and political interference. For instance, the Spanish agency (Comision del Sistema Electrico Nacional), while formally independent, is mainly a consultative body attached to the Ministry of Industry and Energy. Independent regulators endowed with decision-making powers are frequent in the Anglo-Saxon world, in some Latin American countries such as Brazil and Chile, and in several European countries that are committed to introducing institutional innovation in the regulation of electricity.

From this preliminary description of the regulatory settings around the world, a regulatory index (REGULATION) has been constructed for each country; REGULATION takes the value three when a country's regulatory setting entails: (i) regulated TPA; (ii) a 'pool' or a regulated wholesale market for electricity; and (iii) an independent regulatory agency. The higher the index, the more pervasive the regulation and the more competitive the electricity market is likely to be.

Next, the relationship between a country's regulatory index and the quantity and quality of its privatization is determined. This is done by statistically testing various hypotheses about the effect of regulation on privatizing utilities. The first hypothesis is that a more regulated environment should facilitate state sell-offs, because players operate under more competitive regimes in well-regulated settings. Efficiency losses due to natural monopolies are considerably reduced, which increases the political feasibility of infrastructure privatization. A positive correlation between REGULATION and ELSALES is therefore expected.

Second, the regulation index is correlated with aggregate proceeds from privatization in the electricity market (ELREVENUES). Conventional theory suggests that regulation decreases the expected profitability of investment in a privatized firm, given that the firm will operate in a more competitive environment post-privatization. If regulation curbs above-normal profits, investors should insist on paying less for corporate assets in highly regulated settings. But a correlation in the opposite direction cannot be excluded, since clearly established rules reduce uncertainty about future regulatory intervention. Regulatory risk is particularly important for investors in the electric sector, where stranded assets and long-term contracts are common characteristics of firms and transactions (Helm and Jenkinson 1998).

Finally, regulation can serve as a substitute for public ownership of a natural monopoly. The public provision of infrastructure is reasonable, given the possible negative consequences for the taxpayer of private ownership of natural monopolies. This is precisely the reason that government ownership is often recommended by constitutions. But effective regulation may avoid the distributive effects of privatization, allowing governments to privatize larger stakes and eventually relinquish control. To test the effect of regulation on corporate governance in privatized firms, the regulation index was correlated with the quality measure, the cumulative percentage of privatized stock (*ELSTOCK*).[5]

6.6. EMPIRICAL RESULTS

Tables 6.2 to 6.5 display the empirical results. Since many countries did not privatize electricity generation, the dependent variable contains many zeros. Even in these cases, market structure or weak regulation may help to interpret the absence of privatization. Under these circumstances, *OLS* regressions would probably yield downward biased results. Tobit models were therefore used in the empirical analyses at the country level. In contrast, the quality variable at the company level, i.e., the cumulative stake sold in electricity generators (*ELSTOCK*)— is always positive and assumed continuous. *OLS* estimation is therefore more appropriate. Tables 6.2 and 6.3 show the results for the *ELSALES* regressions with vertical integration and regulation as independent variables respectively. Estimation using the two variables in the same equation is impossible due to co-linearity problems.

Table 6.3 shows that vertical integration is strongly negatively correlated with the number of sales in the electricity sector. The coefficient of the *VINT* variable is significant and relatively stable in different specifications, controlling for country-specific effects. This evidence confirms that the presence of a vertically integrated system is a considerable obstacle to electricity privatization.

As stated above, vertically integrated operators should be separated before privatization to avoid the distortions of private ownership of a natural monopoly. Separating generation, which is the potentially competitive part of the business, from transmission and distribution should reduce the likelihood of cross-subsidization within the company. This explains why frequency of sales is

---

[5] In the empirical analysis that we have presented, several variables have been used to control for country-specific effects. The average annual consumption of electricity in kWh for the period that goes from 1977 to 1996 (*CONSUMPTION*) was used to control the size of demand in a given country. Consumption is highly correlated with GDP (correlation 0.95). Thus, *CONSUMPTION* was also used to control for the size of the country. This variable is spurious as a measure of the supply side of the market, given that many countries import electricity. Nevertheless, given that in larger countries the electricity sector may also be larger, the inclusion of this variable allows account to be taken of the supply side effects of privatization. The analysis also includes the political orientation of a country's privatization by the dummy *RIGHT*, the institutional credibility index, given by scores in terms of rule of law, risk of expropriation and contract repudiation by government (*CREDIBILITY*), and the financial market liquidity indicators (*FLOAT* and *TURNOVER*). Variables used in the current authors' earlier work are used to explain the quantity and quality of privatization, and to determine whether they also have an impact in the electricity sector. (For more detailed definitions of the above mentioned variables, see Appendix 1, Data and Methodology.)

Table 6.2. *Privatization in the electricity sector, regulation, and vertical integration*

Country	El sales	El revenue	Agency	Pool	T.P.A	Regulation	Vertical integration
Argentina	14	2,011.12	1	1	1	3	0
Australia	6	9,570.29	1	1	1	3	0
Austria	2	564.94	0	0	0	0	1
Belgium	0	0	0	0	1	1	1
Brazil	2	803.54	1	0	0	1	1
Canada	1	674.94	1	0	0	1	1
Chile	2	538.76	1	1	1	3	0
Colombia	2	936.93	0	1	1	2	0
Denmark	0	0	0	0	1	1	1
England and Wales	3	9,547.12	1	1	1	3	0
Finland	1	429.97	1	1	1	3	0
France	0	0	0	0	0	0	1
Germany	2	548.95	0	0	0	0	1
Greece	0	0	0	0	0	0	1
India	0	0	1	0	0	1	1
Indonesia	0	0	0	0	1	1	1
Ireland	0	0	0	0	0	0	1
Israel	0	0	1	0	0	1	1
Italy	0	0	1	0	0	1	1
Japan	0	0	0	0	0	0	1
Malaysia	0	0	0	0	0	0	0
Mexico	0	0	1	0	1	2	0
Netherlands	0	0	0	0	1	1	0
New Zealand	1	33.5	0	1	0	1	0
Northern Ireland	3	575.95	1	0	1	2	0
Norway	0	0	1	1	1	3	0
Pakistan	1	214.98	0	0	0	0	0
Peru	3	685.94	0	0	1	1	0
Philippines	0	0	1	0	0	1	1
Portugal	1	1,162.9	1	0	0	1	1
Scotland	2	5,384.48	1	0	1	2	1
Singapore	0	0	–	–	–	–	–
South Africa	0	0	1	0	0	1	1
South Korea	0	0	0	0	0	0	1
Spain	1	5,609.55	0	1	1	2	0
Sri Lanka	0	0	–	–	–	–	–
Sweden	0	0	1	1	1	3	0
Switzerland	0	0	0	0	0	0	0
Thailand	1	179.98	0	0	0	0	1
USA	1	55.99	1	1	1	3	0
Venezuela	0	0	0	0	0	0	1

Source: Fondazione Eni Enrico Mattei.

Table 6.3. *Privatization sales in electricity generation (Tobit)*

The dependent variable ELSALES is given by the total number of transactions reported in electricity generation for the 1977–96 period. a, b, and c denote statistical significance at 1, 5, and 10 per cent level, respectively. Standard errors in brackets.

Independent variables	[1]	[2]
CONSTANT	− 3.65 (1.50)[b]	−0.12 (1.34)
VERTICAL INTEGRATION		−3.70[b] (1.39)
REGULATION	1.82[b] (0.57)	
CONSUMPTION	− 0.32E–06 (0.13E–05)	0.45E–06 (0.14E–05)
RIGHT	2.02 (1.34)	2.67[c] (1.50)
σ	3.32[b] (0.58)	3.54[a] (0.62)
No. observations	37	37
Log likelihood	−60.47	−61.75

Table 6.4. *Privatization revenue in electricity generation (Tobit)*

The dependent variable ELREVENUES is given by the total revenues (in US$1996 million) reported in the electricity generation for the 1977–96 period. a, b ,and c denote statistical significance at 1, 5, and 10 per cent level, respectively. Standard errors in brackets.

Independent variables	[1]	[2]
CONSTANT	−3578.33[b] (1238.28)	39.93 (1210.67)
VERTICAL INTEGRATION		−2526.88[b] (1419.47)
REGULATION	1830.89[b] (541.47)	
CONSUMPTION	−0.18E–02 (0.13E–02)	−0.82E–03 (0.15E–02)
FLOAT	7970.38[c] (4116.34)	6109.54 (4721.75)
σ	3093.21[b] (542.63)	3661.78[b] (649.12)
No. observations	35	35
Log likelihood	−179.95	−183.49

Source: Fondazione Eni Enrico Mattei.

lower in electricity markets dominated by a single vertically integrated player. In several circumstances, the incumbent, with its large corporate assets, is powerful and can invest resources in the political market to avoid liberalization. Thus, only a government strong enough to counterbalance this pressure to keep the *status quo* can implement unbundling. Accordingly, vertical integration is an important determinant of the speed of a privatization process.

Table 6.3 provides evidence of the effects of regulation on the variable ELSALES.

The regulatory index REGULATION is highly significant, positive, and stable in different specifications. The regression presented is representative of many others. The frequency of sales in the electricity sector is therefore highly positively correlated with the extent of regulation. This result is easily explained. If a well-defined regulatory framework is in place at the time of the sale, privatization will be easier for governments; if the market is liberalized in the segments where competition is viable and appropriately regulated where natural monopoly-type bottlenecks exist, supernormal profits will be curbed. A well-designed privatization package, including liberalization and regulation, will therefore be more politically acceptable. If clear rules exist, privatization can smoothly enter the second stage involving utilities such as electricity.

The control variable CONSUMPTION is not significant in either of the regressions presented in Tables 6.3 and Table 6.4 This indicates that the scope of a country's privatization in the electricity sector is virtually independent of electricity demand. In contrast, the political dummy RIGHT is significant and positive. The results in the earlier work of the present authors suggested that conservative majorities appear to be more involved in the privatization of strategic sectors such as electricity.

It is not surprising that vertical integration and regulation have an impact on the speed of divestiture of state assets. The countries that have successfully privatized have also deeply restructured and liberalized the electricity sector before privatization. The economic effects of vertical integration and regulation upon the proceeds from sales in the electricity sector is more controversial.

As stated above, some argue that liberalization and regulation reduce the expected profitability of the investment, so that bidders should not be willing to pay as much for assets in the electricity business in highly regulated settings. Others contend that regulatory risk also has an impact at the time of the sale. Investors may discount the possibility of unexpected regulation or government decisions by policymakers, as happened in the case of the MCC intervention in the BP case.

The results shown in Table 6.4 provide some tentative answers to these important questions. In all the regressions presented, the higher the regulatory index, the higher are the aggregate proceeds from sales in the electricity sector. In particular, a one-point increase in the index raises revenue of approximately $1.8 billion. Regulatory risk, therefore, seems to have a substantial impact. No statistically significant relation is present either with respect to the turnover ratio or the institutional credibility variable (CREDIBILITY). The second financial market development indicator (FLOAT) is, instead, positively related to the privatization proceeds, indicating a possible role for liquidity on the financial success of the issues.

These results with respect to the effects of regulation on privatization proceeds can be interpreted within the framework of incomplete contracting (Coase 1937; Hart and Moore 1988). Buying a utility is akin to signing a contract with the government. In the privatization transaction, parties are called upon to strike this contract with limited information concerning future contingencies. Under these circumstances, regulation reduces uncertainty and therefore transaction costs. Clear rules, appropriately enforced, help bidders to gauge more precisely the expected profitability of the investment, which increases their willingness to

Table 6.5. *The percentage of capital sold in electricity generation (OLS)*

The dependent variable ELSTOCK is given by the cumulative stake sold in electricity generators for the 1977–96 period. a, b, and c denote statistical significance at 1, 5, and 10 per cent level, respectively. Heteroskedastic-consistent standard errors in brackets.

Independent variables	Dependent variable: ElStock	
CONSTANT	63.7^a (9.61)	29.53^c (16.10)
REGULATION	5.71 (3.79)	6.62^c (3.64)
CONSUMPTION	–	0.60E–05 (0.10E–04)
CREDIBILITY	–	4.27^b (1.78)
No. observations	48	48
Adj. R^2	0.04	0.14

Source: Fondazione Eni Enrico Mattei.

pay. In contrast, the absence of a well-defined regulatory framework increases transaction costs, because rational investors will discount for the possibility that government may change the rules of the game *ex post*. The consequences of such an act can be particularly severe in electricity, where long-term investment and stranded assets are intrinsic characteristics of the market.[6]

The quality of a privatization process can be evaluated based on the size of the stake sold. In utilities, and particularly electricity, an important issue is whether regulation affects the willingness of governments to transfer ownership and relinquish control to privatized firms.

In Table 6.5 a regression for ELSTOCK has been run using the regulatory index of the country in which the privatized company operates, and some control variables at the country level. A major flaw in these estimates is that due to the lack of data, there is no control of firm-specific fixed effects. Although preliminary, the results in Table 6.5 indicate a clear positive and statistically significant correlation between the regulatory index and the stake sold. The coefficient remains stable and significant when account is taken of country-specific effects, whereas the controls are never significant.[7]

---

[6] Auction theory provides a normative interpretation of this result. The government typically enjoys superior information about the regulatory environment in which the firm will operate. Adoption of regulation makes it publicly accessible and verifiable. If the bidders' valuations are correlated, expected revenues for governments will increase in all standard auctions (Milgrom and Weber 1982; Schmidt and Schnitzer 1997).

[7] It may be argued that endogeneity problems may affect these results. The degree of privatization could determine market structure, as a de-integrated regime can be the outcome of privatization. The variable VINT is nonetheless defined as a dummy for the presence of a vertically integrated system. It is less evident that vertical integration is endogenous to the degree of privatization. Similarly, it may be argued that liberalization, regulation, and privatization are all parts of a structural reform package and simultaneously implemented. This is seldom true. Rather, the results show that in the electricity sector, with few exceptions (i.e. Spain), regulation is typically followed by the privatization decree. Hausman tests have been used to check for possible simultaneity, and the results were mixed. Nevertheless, the results are more supportive of the hypothesis of exogeneity of the variables of interest.

Regulation not only influences the quantity of state assets sold in the electric industry, as confirmed by the results from the sales and revenue estimated, but may also shrink the residual stake held by the government. This evidence has strong implications for corporate governance in utilities. Although it represents a second-best solution, regulation may provide a partial substitute for public ownership to achieve allocative efficiency (see Schmidt 1996). Benevolent governments will privatize larger stakes if shareholders will not reap surpluses via excessive dividends at the expense of consumers. But privatization will not be equivalent to public ownership, as it will enhance productive efficiency. Under these conditions, privatization combined with suitable regulation should generate large efficiency gains.

6.7. CONCLUSIONS

This chapter attempts to single out some critical influences affecting privatization in monopolistic industries. It focuses upon two factors that may influence the pace of divestiture in network industries: vertical integration and regulation. The results are straightforward. First, vertical integration of a system substantially reduces the frequency of utility sales. Second, regulation appears to be crucial for the success of privatization in the utility sector. The regulatory indicators correlate strongly with the quantity of sales of electricity, the size of the stake sold, and the revenue from sales. As the theory suggests, the public-monopoly-turns-into-private-monopoly argument does not apply in well-regulated settings. Consequently, an important rationale for public ownership of natural monopolies loses relevance. This reasoning explains not only the low number of sales and percentage of stock sold in poorly regulated electricity markets, but also why sales are less frequent where vertically integrated players dominate the market.

Regulation does not appear to decrease the revenue generated by the sale of public enterprises, although it can reduce the expected profitability of the firm curbing supernormal profits. However, it provides clear rules and a framework in which investments and business opportunities can be more effectively gauged. The regressions in this study indicate that the latter factor dominates the former in investors' decision-making. Governments should therefore not be wary of regulating first and then privatizing.

Conclusion

At this juncture, it is natural to draw some conclusions from our work. Instead of summarizing the main results obtained, we will present our reflections on what we consider the two most important findings of the book.

The first is a stylized fact at the macroeconomic level. Privatization is one of the main events of the economic and financial history of the twentieth century. However, at the turn of the century, the process abruptly slowed down, and actually appears a spent force both in developed and in less developed economies.

The second is a finding at the microeconomic level. Privatization has been partial and incomplete. In developed economies, it mostly involved the floating of the company shares in the stock market. In less developed countries, it took the form of strategic partnership with foreign operators. However, in most cases privatization did not entail a dramatic change in governance structures, as private ownership and public control seem to coexist.

These findings beg two fundamental questions, which this book tries to address. The first is the following. Is privatization a long-term trend proceeding in parallel with the advance of market capitalism, or rather a cycle following the short- or medium-term fluctuations of economic fundamentals?

The economic model of privatization that we developed in this book suggests that privatization processes are shaped by economic and political determinants. Particularly, they are affected by economic outlook and market conditions, so that large privatization waves are systematically associated with economic growth and bull stock markets. But political preferences and budget constraints also matter. Indeed market oriented governments in financial distress appear more eager to privatize.

The actual stalemate and the above considerations suggest that the big privatization wave of the 1980s and especially the 1990s has mostly been a cyclical phenomenon, where the engines of sales have been economic growth, booming stock markets, and worsening fiscal conditions. The same model described above forecasts that a new large-scale privatization cycle could start as soon as the economy recovers from the actual depression. Indeed, governments have property left to sell.

The second question is related to the last observation. Is partial privatization a snapshot of a process in motion, or rather a stable outcome? In other words, is the coexistence of private ownership with public control just a transient anomaly, or a functional pattern of governance?

This is certainly a more difficult question, and our book cannot provide any clear-cut answer to it, due especially to lack of data. However, we have shown that genuine privatization (i.e. the transfer of ownership and control to the private sector) is difficult to achieve and sustain as several conditions must be met. First, markets should be competitive or suitably regulated. Second, private investors should be adequately protected by the law in order to avoid expropriation. Third, political institutions should be designed to limit the veto power of constituencies ousting full divestiture. Last but not least, governments should be credibly committed not to interfere post-privatization in the operating activity of the companies.

This long list of conditions is certainly prohibitive and it also explains why genuine privatization is found only among a group of countries around the world. Certainly, the United Kingdom may represent the closest approximation to this ideal model. However, even where privatization has been pushed to the full extent, the government hangs on to control important parts of the national economy by the use of golden shares or similar mechanisms.

From this perspective, finding the private-ownership-public-control pattern as the dominant form of governance in several privatized firms is not particularly surprising. It simply witnesses the difficulty of implementing the structural reforms needed to fully garner the benefits of privatization.

If we combine these two main stylized facts at the macro and micro level and the respective explanations, we can formulate our view about future privatization trends. Global economic recovery is likely to push the process towards a fresh start. However, the stage of increasing returns of privatization is probably over, as companies in competitive sectors have already been privatized and the newly privatized sectors require careful regulation and market design. Furthermore, the stakes sold in strategic sectors begin to be critical for the contestability of corporate control. And governments of all political stripes are wary of relinquishing the control of SOEs in poorly regulated environments.

For these reasons, private ownership tied to public control is probably not a stable equilibrium outcome, but it is very likely to persist in the near future. This does not mean that Adam Smith's lessons about the efficiency of private property are no longer valid. Rather, that they are very difficult to put into practice—hence the title of our book.

Appendix 1: Data and Methodology

The empirical analyses are based on a series of international data sets which have been constructed at the Fondazione Eni Enrico Mattei, and contain several privatization, economic, financial, political, and institutional data, mainly for the period 1977–2001.

In this appendix we will describe how the variables have been constructed, and their sources.

1. Privatization Variables

The primary sources of our privatization data are *Privatization International* and *Securities Data Corporation*,[1] reporting globally 3,535 transactions worth over $127 billion (current as of 2001) in 140 countries.

Our sources report information at the transaction level about the type of privatization (PO or PS). The data for each privatization carried out by private sale or public offer include the date of the deal, the company's industrial sector and country, the total value of the transaction (in current US$ million), the per cent for sale, and other qualitative information. In the sample group, the maximum value recorded for a single operation is around $40 billion (current), while the minimum is $100,000 for an average of $306 million.

2. Political Variables

In order to test the political theories, we need data about the partisan dimension of privatization. In particular, we want to identify the political orientation of privatizing governments over time.

In this direction, we have retrieved the political history of the forty-nine countries in the La Porta *et al.* (1998) sample from the Banks *et al.* 1997 edition of the *Political Handbook of the World*. This source reports election dates, dates of appointment of the cabinets, and a description of political systems around the world up to 1997. We updated this information for the years 1998–99 by use of Internet sources mentioned in the detailed definitions of the political variables.

We then used Wilfried Derksen's *Electoral Web Sites* and classification system to label incumbent governments, considering the platform and ideological orientation of the supporting parties. Four possible categories are identified: (i) democratic conservative (right wing); (ii) centrist and Christian-democratic; (iii) democratic left wing; (iv) non-democratic.

---

[1] In April 1998, *Privatisation International* merged with *IFR Platinum* of Thomson Financial, a leading provider of financial data. From 2001, all the transactions reported in IFR-Platinum are also contained in *Securities Data Corporation*.

Appendix 1: Data and Methodology

Table A1.1. *Privatization variables*

Variable	Definition	Source
ABROAD	Percentage of privatized stock placed on non-domestic financial markets (flag Rule 144a included). The variable refers to each single PO.	*Privatisation International*, and *Securities Data Corporation*.
ELREVENUES	Aggregate revenues from total operations in electricity generation per country 1977–97 (US$1996mil).	*Privatisation International*, and *Securities Data Corporation*.
ELSALES	Total number of operations by Public Offer (PO) and Private Sales (PS) in electricity generation per country 1977–97.	*Privatisation International*, and *Securities Data Corporation*.
ELSTOCK	Cumulative stake sold in electricity generators at the firm level.	*Privatisation International*, and *Securities Data Corporation*.
ENERGY	Dummy taking the value 1 when the privatized company belongs to the following sectors: electricity (generation), oil and gas production.	*Privatisation International*, and *Securities Data Corporation*.
FINANCE	Dummy taking the value 1 when the privatized company belongs to the following sectors: banking, financial intermediation, insurance.	*Privatisation International*, and *Securities Data Corporation*.
IPO	Dummy taking the value 1 when the Share Issue Privatization (SIP) is an Initial Public Offer (IPO).	*Privatisation International*, and *Securities Data Corporation*.
PO/DEALS	Ratio of the number of Public Offers (PO) to the total number of privatizations implemented in the period 1977–2001.	*Privatisation International*, and *Securities Data Corporation*.
PO/SALES	Ratio of the number of Public Offers (PO) to the total number of sales implemented in the period 1977–1996.	
PRIVAMV	Market value of privatized firms.	Elaboration on *Datastream*.
PRIVATRADE	Value of trades of privatized firms.	Elaboration on *Datastream*.
REV/GDP	Ratio of total revenue (in US$1995mil) cumulated in the period to 2000 GDP (in US$1995mil).	*Securities Data Corporation and World Bank, World Development Indicators* (2002).

Table A1.1. (*Cont.*)

Variable	Definition	Source
REV/GDP	Total revenues from privatization to Gross Domestic Product in country *i* in year *t*. Total revenues are revenues in current US$ from total privatization deals (PO and PS). Gross Domestic Product is expressed in current US$.	*Privatisation International Database, IFR Thomson Database, World Development Indicators.*
REVENUES	Aggregate revenues from privatizations during the period 1977–2001, in US$1995mil per country.	*Privatisation International*, and *Securities Data Corporation.*
SIZE/CAP	Ratio of the implied market value of the company (SIZE: obtained by dividing total revenues from the SIP by the percentage of capital privatized, multiplied by 100) in current US$ to the market capitalization in the year of the SIP.	*Privatisation International, IFC Emerging Stock Markets Factbook 1999, Federation International des Bourse des Valeurs (FIBV).*
STOCK	Average percentage of capital sold by company over the period 1977–2001 per country.	*Privatisation International*, and *Securities Data Corporation.*
TLC	Dummy taking the value 1 when the privatized company belongs to the telecommunications sector.	*Privatisation International*, and *Securities Data Corporation.*
TRANSACTIONS OR DEALS	Total number of privatizations by Public Offer (PO) and Private Sale (PS) (tranches or complete sales) implemented in the period 1977–2001.	*Privatisation International*, and *Securities Data Corporation.*
UTILITY	Dummy taking the value 1 when the privatized company belongs to the following sectors: airline, airport, electricity distribution, gas distribution, rail services, rail track, water and sewage.	*Privatisation International*, and *Securities Data Corporation.*
WSTOCK	Weighted average percentage of capital sold over all firms, where the weights are given by the ratios between the revenues from privatization, by PO and PS, and total revenues in country *i* in year *t*.	*Privatisation International*, and *Securities Data Corporation.*

Appendix 1: Data and Methodology

Table A1.2. *Economic and financial variables*

Variable	Definition	Source
AVDEFICIT	Country average of the public sector Deficit as a percentage of GDP in the three years before each SIP.	*World Development Indicators, International Financial Statistics.*
AVGROWTH	Average annual rate of growth of GDP per capita for the period 1977–1996.	*World Development Indicators* (1995).
CAP	Stock market capitalization to Gross Domestic Product in country *i* at year *t*. Stock market capitalization in year *t* is calculated as the average between the end-of-year market capitalization deflated by the end-of-year Consumer Price Index in year *t* and *t* − 1. Stock market capitalization refers to a country's main stock exchange.	Beck, Demirgüç-Kunt, and Levine (1999), updated using data from *IFC, Emerging Stock Markets Factbook*, and *FIBV*.
CONSUMPTION	Average consumption of electricity in KwH 1977–96.	*International Energy Agency.*
DEBT	Total debt as a percentage of Gross Domestic Product of country *i* in year *t*. Total debt is expressed as the whole stock of direct, government, fixed term contractual obligations to others outstanding at a particular date. It includes domestic debt (such as debt held by monetary authorities, deposit money banks, non-financial public enterprises, and households) and foreign debt (such as debt to international development institutions and foreign governments).	*International Financial Statistics.*
DEFICIT	Average deficit of central government for the three years prior to the first privatization.	*World Bank* (1995).
FLOAT	Total value of trades on the major stock exchange/GDP.	*World Development Indicators.*
GDP	The logarithm of GDP US$1995.	*World Bank, World Development Indicators* (2002).
GDP PER CAPITA	Ratio of Gross Domestic Product in constant US$ 1996 to population in country *i* in year *t*. Total population counts all residents regardless of legal status or citizenship.	*World Development Indicators, World Bank, International Financial Statistics.*

Table A1.2. (*Cont.*)

Variable	Definition	Source
GROWTH	Annual percentage growth rate of Gross Domestic Product at market prices based on constant local currency in country *i* in year *t*. Aggregates are based on constant 1995 US$.	*World Development Indicators,* and *http://www.worldbank.org.*
LOG OF GNP	Log of the average Gross National Product (1977–1996).	*World Bank, World Development Indicators* (1995).
MV	Monthly total market capitalization.	Elaboration on *Datastream*
SOE	Degree of importance of the public company in a state's economy in the year before the first privatization. Average of: (i) ratio between the value-added of the SOE and GDP; (ii) SOE employment as a percentage of the total work force; (iii) SOE gross investment on total investment, (where available).	*World Bank* (1995).
TRADE	Monthly total trading value.	Elaboration on *Datastream.*
TURNOVER	Stock market total value traded to total market capitalization in a country in year *t*. Total market value in year *t* is deflated by the Consumer Price Index in year *t*. Market capitalization in year *t* is calculated as the average between the end-of-year market capitalization deflated by the end-of-year Consumer Price Index in year *t* and *t* − 1. Trading value and market capitalization refer to a country's main stock exchange.	*IFC Emerging Stock Markets Factbook 1999, Federation International des Bourse des Valeurs (FIBV).*

Appendix 1: Data and Methodology

Table A1.3. *Political variables*

Variable	Definition	Source
CENTRE	Dummy variable taking the value 1 when the incumbent executive in country i in year t was supported by 'centrist' parties, and 0 otherwise. This label includes parties which are in the centre of the political spectrum without officially adhering to free market values, Christian-democratic parties, and wide coalitional governments without a clearly discernible orientation.	Banks *et al.* (1997), *Wilfried Derksen's Electoral Web Sites (www.agora.stm.it/elections), Zarate's World Political Leaders 1945–2001 (www.terra.es/ personal2/monolith), Library of Congress Country Studies (http:// lcweb2.loc.gov/frd/cs/cshome.html).*
DISPR	Disproportionality index. Sum of absolute differences between electoral votes share and seats share, for all the parties. Such divergence usually means overrepresentation of major parties and partial or complete exclusion of minor ones. Thus, increasing values of the index accord to the majoritarian rule, lower values to the proportional one.	Original dataset from Lijphart, updated using *Electoral Studies*, various years; Banks *et al.* (1997); *Elections around the World; Parties and Elections in Europe; Political Reference Almanac.*
ELECTION	Dummy variable taking the value 1 on the year of a country's elections, and zero otherwise. In presidential systems, presidential elections are considered. In parliamentary systems, general elections are considered.	Banks *et al.* (1997), *Wilfried Derksen's Electoral Web Sites* (Persson and Tabellini, 2001).
ENP	Concentration index computed over parties seats shares in the legislative chamber.	Original dataset from Lijphart, updated using *Electoral Studies*, various years; Banks *et al.* (1997); *Elections around the World; Parties and Elections in Europe; Political Reference Almanac.*
LEFT	Dummy variable taking the value 1 when the incumbent executive in country i in year t was supported by 'left-wing parties' and 0 otherwise. Left-wing parties include labour, socialist, social-democratic, and communist parties.	Banks *et al.* (1997), *Wilfried Derksen's Electoral Web Sites (www.agora.stm.it/elections), Zarate's World Political Leaders 1945–2001 (www.terra.es/ personal2/monolith), Library of Congress Country Studies (http:// lcweb2.loc.gov/frd/cs/cshome.html).*

Table A1.3. (*Cont.*)

Variable	Definition	Source
MWOP	Discrete measure which accounts for the type of government in office: one party, minimal winning, minimal winning–one party, or neither of them.	Original dataset from Lijphart, updated using *Electoral Studies*, various years; Banks *et al.* (1997); *Elections Around the World (www.electionworld.org); Parties and Elections in Europe (www. parties-and-elections.de/ indexe. html), Political Reference Almanac (http://www.polisci.com/ almanac/nations.htm).*
NONDEM	Dummy taking the value 1 when the privatization was implemented by a dictatorial, military, or authoritarian ruler.	Wilfried Derksen's *Electoral Web Site.*
PARTISAN	Indicator for the government's partisanship. It is computed as the weighted average of the score attached to parties forming the government coalition, according to Huber and Inglehart (1995) and it ranges from 0 to 10. Weight i-th equal the number of seats held by party i-th in the legislative chamber over the total held by the government coalition. Null weight is assigned to parties whose seats are not essential for the government coalition to hold the absolute majority.	*Electoral Studies,* various years, Banks *et al.* (1997), *Zarate's World Political Leaders since 1945 (www.terra.es/ personal2/monolith), Library of Congress Country Studies (http:// lcweb2.loc.gov/frd/cs/cshome.html), Administration and Cost of Elections (www.aceproject. org), Elections Around the World (www. electionworld.org) Parties and Elections in Europe (www.parties- and-elections.de/indexe.html), Political Reference Almanac (http:// www.polisci.com/almanac/ nations.htm).*
POLINST	Standardized mean of the three measures *DISPR, ENP,* and *MWOP.* The standardization is performed over the whole sample.	
RIGHT	Dummy variable taking the value 1 when the incumbent executive in country *i* in year *t* was supported by 'democratic-conservative parties', and 0 otherwise. Democratic conservative parties are defined as parties adhering to traditional values in combination with free-market ideology and law-and-order positions.	Banks *et al.* (1997), *Wilfried Derksen's Electoral Web Sites (www.agora.stm.it/elections), Zarate's World Political Leaders 1945–2001 (www.terra.es/ personal2/monolith), Library of Congress Country Studies (http:// lcweb2.loc.gov/frd/cs/cshome.html).*
RIGHTGOV	Dummy variable taking value 1 for Scandinavian civil law countries, and 0 otherwise.	La Porta *et al.* (1998).

Appendix 1: Data and Methodology

Table A1.4. *Institutional variables*

Variable	Definition	Source
AGENCY	Dummy taking the value 1 when an independent agency as regulatory institution is present.	Lewington (1997).
ANTIDIRECTOR	Index that measures the legal protection that a country's company law provides against the risk of expropriation by managers. The variable takes into account the existence by law of (i) proxy voting by mail, (ii) cumulative voting for directors, (iii) oppressed minority mechanisms, (iv) requirements about the deposit of shares prior to general share holders meeting, (v) minimum percentage of shares to call for an extraordinary meeting at 10 per cent or below, and (vi) the pre-emptive rights that can be waived only by a shareholder's vote. It ranges from 0 to 6.	La Porta *et al.* (1998).
COMMON LAW	Variable that takes the value of 1 if a country belongs to the common law legal tradition and 0 otherwise. It never explicitly appears in estimates together with other legal traditions as this would cause problems of co-linearity with the constant. It is, therefore, the implicit benchmark with which the influence of other legal traditions is compared. In our sample group, the common law countries are: the United Kingdom, the United States, Australia, Canada, Hong Kong, India, Ireland, Israel, Kenya, Malaysia, New Zealand, Nigeria, Pakistan, Singapore, South Africa, Sri Lanka, Thailand, Zimbabwe.	La Porta *et al.* (1998).
CREDIBILITY	Average grade in terms of risk of contract repudiation and risk of expropriation in country i in year t. It ranges from 0 to 10.	*International Country Risk Guide.*
FRENCH LAW	Variable that takes the value of 1 if a country belongs to the French Civil Law tradition and 0 otherwise. In our sample group, the countries belonging to this tradition are: France, Argentina, Belgium, Brazil, Chile, Columbia, Ecuador, Egypt, Greece, Indonesia, Italy, Jordan, Mexico, Holland, Peru, the Philippines, Portugal, Spain, Turkey, Uruguay, Venezuela.	La Porta *et al.* (1998).

Table A1.4. (*Cont.*)

Variable	Definition	Source
GERMAN-SCANDINAVIAN LAW	Variable that takes the value of 1 if a country belongs to the German–Scandinavian Civil Law tradition and 0 otherwise. In our sample group, the countries belonging to this tradition are: Austria, Germany, Switzerland, Japan, South Korea, Taiwan, Denmark, Finland, Norway, Sweden.	La Porta *et al.* (1998).
POOL	Dummy taking the value 1 when a wholesale electricity market ('pool') is operational.	Lewington (1997).
REGULATION	Regulatory index taking the value 3 when AGENCY, POOL, and TPA dummies are present.	Lewington (1997).
TPA	Dummy taking the value 1 when Regulated Third Party Access is granted by law.	Lewington (1997).
VINT	Dummy taking the value 1 when a vertically integrated electric system is present.	Lewington (1997).

When the ideological orientation of a government remained unclear (due to frequent party changes and mergers in countries such as Turkey, Peru, Pakistan, and South Korea), we referred to the description of the political settings and institutions by the Federal Research Division of the Library of Congress of the United States. This source also allowed us to classify the most controversial cases.

In order to identify correctly the political preferences of the incumbent governments, we distinguish *presidential* and *parliamentary* systems. In the former, we considered the political orientation of the president's party and his cabinet; in the latter, the political orientation of the parliamentary majority supporting the cabinet. By the same token, in order to identify political switches, we consider presidential elections in presidential systems, and general elections—or simple changes of parliamentary majorities—in parliamentary systems. Determining whether political systems are presidential or not depends on answering a number of questions: following Persson and Tabellini (2001), we choose to check first whether the executive depends on a parliamentary majority; second if the president is elected by direct popular vote or with a *de facto* similar method of choice (like the US system), and he forms and leads the cabinet appointing and dismissing ministers (including the prime minister, if this office is present); and third (in those few cases where the political system is still uncertain of classification) whether the president is the most important decision-maker, holding the core of the executive power. We considered presidential ballots and parliamentary majorities only in France, a presidential country which is customarily considered parliamentary in cases of 'cohabitation'. 'Cohabitation' occurs when the president loses the parliamentary majority support and must abandon the reality of power to the prime minister if a party other than his own ever has a majority in the National Assembly (Aron 1982).

We have to attribute a political label to each country-year. When we observed a change in a government's political orientation after elections or (in parliamentary regimes) during the same legislature, we matched the political data with the dates of privatization sales. We attributed the political label to the government implementing the majority of the sales in the year. For example, a political switch from a centrist to a right-wing majority occurs in Italy in May 1994: five deals out of nine were implemented by the newly elected government in 1994, so we attached the label 'right wing' to that year. When a tie occurred, we used the (current) dollar amount of revenue to discriminate. For example, in France after the 1997 elections in June, the newly elected left-wing government implemented the same number of sales (two) of the former right-wing government. The left-wing government raised 93 per cent of the total revenue of that year, so we attached the left-wing label to France in 1997.

This methodology allows us to attach unambiguously one of the political dummies (i.e. *right wing, centre, left wing, non dem*) to each country-year.

3. The Control Sample

The rules for identifying the matching firms for our sample of privatized companies are as follows.

Table A1.5. *Industrial sectors*

Sectors	SIC numbers
Petroleum industry	13, 29
Finance/Real Estate industry	60–69
Consumer durables industry	25, 30, 36, 37, 50, 55, 57
Basic industry	10, 12, 14, 24, 26, 28, 33
Food/tobacco industry	1, 9, 20, 21, 54
Construction industry	15–17, 32, 52
Capital goods industry	34, 35, 38
Transportation industry	40–42, 44, 45, 47
Utilities industry	46, 48, 49
Textiles/trade industry	22, 23, 31, 51, 53, 56, 59
Services industry	72, 73, 75, 80, 82, 87, 89
Leisure industry	27, 58, 70, 78, 79

Source: Campbell (1996).

Table A1.6. *Control sample*

Criteria	Total	Percentage
Number of companies	143	100
Best case	78	54.54
Second-best case	64	44.75
Third-best case	1	0.69

Source: Fondazione Eni Enrico Mattei.

- *Best case.* We first match by country. A sample of size greater than or equal to 1 passes this screen. Within this sample, we next match by industry. As to the industry classification, we use the Campbell (1996) system based on two-digits SIC numbers (see Table A1.5). A sub-sample of size greater than or equal to 1 passes this second screen. We sort this sub-sample by market capitalization, and choose the private firm with the market capitalization closest to our privatized firm within the 30 per cent range.
- *Second-best case.* If we do not find any match in the country, we first match by industry. A sample of size greater than or equal to 1 passes this screen. Then we pick up an international firm in the same sector with the market capitalization closest to our privatized firm in the 30 per cent range.
- *Third-best case.* We do this if we do not obtain the best case or the second-best case. We first match by country. A sample of size greater than or equal to 1 passes this screen. Then we pick up the domestic firm with the market capitalization closest to our privatized firm in the 30 per cent range (Table A1.6).

Appendix 2: Importing Investor Protection

Inefficient regulation hinders the development of financial markets and, as a consequence, lowers the chances of a successful privatization programme. The problem is particularly severe in developing and emerging countries where profitable companies may exist but a company's growth potential is limited by the difficulty of attracting external finance, be it debt or equity. International organizations have tried to cope with this market failure by the financing of infrastructure through 'Build-Own-Operate' (BOO) schemes.[1]

A look at more recent operations, however, shows that governments from poorly regulated countries are more often tapping international capital markets as a source of capital. A placement on highly developed markets—like NYSE and NASDAQ or the London Stock Exchange—is now a common practice for the best performing companies. In the majority of cases, the flotation is split into an international and a domestic tranche, sometimes in conjunction with a private equity placement to a core of strategic investors.

The benefits of floating shares in a foreign exchange (the so called 'cross-listing') have been analysed in the financial literature in terms of improved diversification opportunities, enhanced liquidity, and reduction in the cost of capital. However the most convincing explanation seems the one based on improved investor protection. Indeed, by cross-listing shares, national governments 'import' the rules of more advanced markets in that the shareholders of privatized companies benefit from the legal and institutional apparatus that protects foreign investors. Clearly, this binding mechanism has a cost for the controlling shareholder as it limits the possibility of extracting private benefits of control. But projects that require large amounts of outside capital can only be funded if the incentives of controlling shareholders are aligned with those of minority investors. Therefore, cross-listing shares is fundamental for privatized companies that have substantial growth opportunities.

The available empirical data confirms this hunch. Doidge, Karolyi, and Stultz (2001) show the existence of a cross-listing premium for companies listed in the USA, i.e. a valuation differential of 16.5 per cent between the companies listed in the USA and companies from the same countries listed only in the domestic market. Interestingly, the differential increases as firms choose more stringent and prestigious listing mechanisms, as we will describe below.

1. Cross-listing Procedures

To illustrate the economic implications of cross-listing, it is useful to analyse first some technical and institutional aspects of this type of placement. When a company decides to launch a global offer on a major stock exchange, such as NYSE, it usually structures a

---

[1] For a comprehensive analysis of the costs and benefits of these schemes, see Sheshinski and Lòpez-Calva (2000).

Depository Receipt (DR) Programme. DRs are representative securities held in deposit by the country of the issuing company. They are traded in the currency of the host country and subject to its rules regarding clearance, settlement, and the transfer of ownership. These characteristics facilitate the evaluation of stock by international investors and, above all, reduce the transaction costs of investment in a foreign company, bypassing most of the paperwork and tax problems associated with the acquisition of foreign stock (Mustafa and Fink 1998).

There are different types of DR entailing different levels of complexity and disclosure. Global Depository Receipts (GDR) are usually traded in major stock exchanges outside the US–above all on the London Stock Exchange (LSE)–and in over-the-counter markets in the US. A company that issues GDRs is not subject to the General Accepted Accounting Principles (GAAP) nor must it wholly abide by SEC regulations. As a consequence, the issue of GDRs allows a company to enjoy the benefits of international trading without modifying its reporting practices. This may, however, displease some investors.

Companies that intend to offer their shares to American institutional investors and be quoted on US stock markets must use American Depository Receipts (ADR). These entail the same obligations as American shares, ranging from GAAPs to full compliance of SEC rules on transparency.

ADR and GDR programmes are not the only ways in which a foreign company can have access to the American market; one possible alternative is the private placement of DRs under SEC's Rule 144a. This method is the cheapest in that it allows the issuing company to avoid SEC authorization. The rationale for this exemption is that stock issued under Rule 144a is traded in upstairs markets by large institutional investors (the so-called Qualified Institutional Buyers, QIB). QIBs are, in fact, primary financial institutions that, in most cases, are in the position to obtain autonomously key information about stock. Therefore they do not need the same protection that SEC warrants to the public (Rovinescu and Thieffry 1996).

It often happens that global offers are structured using a combination of the above methods. The choice of DR depends on the operation's goals in terms of visibility and on the financial solidity of the issuer. Obviously, ADRs are the most attractive and secure method for foreign investors, but they are also the most costly. Companies for which transaction costs associated with ADRs are deemed excessive can opt for stock market placements under less stringent regulations, such as Rule 144.

Looking at the details of DR operations, the offer usually begins with the appointment of a financial adviser–typically an investment bank–given the task of establishing the number of shares corresponding to one DR (the DR ratio). The aim is to make the nominal value of the security comparable with those quoted on international markets. The consultant then appoints a depository bank to take custody of the securities in the country of the issuing company.

The number of shares and the sale price is usually determined through book-building. Book-building begins with a dialogue between the lead manager and a representative of the underwriters. Potential investors indicate the number of shares they may want to buy within certain price ranges. The offers are not at all binding, but indicative; final prices and quantities are determined considering the intrinsic value of the company and investors' offers. According to traders, book-building is an efficient auctioning method as it allows for a more precise evaluation of the company. In reality, it is not the procedure which guarantees the success of the operation, but the competitiveness of the auction and the choice of the pricing strategy.

Some theoretical and empirical contributions have shown that competitive auctions have a positive impact on prices (Brannman, Douglas, and Weiss 1984; Milgrom 1987). In the context of privatization, recent studies on 236 Mexican operations have further confirmed these results: a high number of bidders generates a significant premium, as does the absence of limits on the participation of foreign investors (Lopéz-de-Silanes 1997).

Some important sales in India clearly show the importance of pricing strategy in the success of placements (Mustafa and Fink 1998). BPL Cellular Holdings is a company that operates in the Indian cellular phone sector. The first ADRs issue at a price of sixteen dollars per share was, in fact, halted only a few hours before the established placement date due to a lack of buyers. Analysts came up with different explanations for this débâcle: first, the majority of investors maintained that the price was too high, only subscribing partially to the offer. To absorb what was left over, the price was dropped to twelve dollars and subsequently to ten dollars per share. These sudden price reductions were read negatively by analysts, and confirmed their concerns over the entire operation. Similarly, the placement of another Indian telecommunications sector group, VSNL, was cancelled on 3 May 1994, following the negative reaction of investors to a sale price of 1,500 rupees when analysts had valued them at 1,000 rupees. Five months later, the government resumed the offer at a price closer to fair value, but the offer was again halted (Guislain 1997). Finally, in March 1997, VSNL managed successfully to place GDRs for a total value of $448 million. The offer was many times oversubscribed. The reasons for the success of the final operation were many, but were mainly due to the effectiveness of the road-show (attracting over 650 institutional investors from twenty-eight countries) and in the choice of a particularly competitive book-building method.

Appendix 3: Golden Shares Around the World

Governments have certainly been creative in granting themselves special powers and imposing statutory constraints over SOEs. As is widely known, the golden (special) share was born in the UK and then spread out in several countries.

This Appendix tries to describe in some detail the institutional complexity of golden shares as a means of keeping control in partially or totally privatized SOEs in a selection of developed countries.

United Kingdom

In the United Kingdom, special shares have a broadly similar content. In general, the prior consent of the special shareholder is required for any change of the limitations in the Articles of Association which usually prevent a person—or persons acting in concert—from having an interest in 15 per cent or more in the voting share capital. The articles defining rights attached to the special share cannot be altered or removed. The special shares do not carry any rights to vote at general meetings but entitle the holder to attend and speak at such meetings. The special share in this 'basic' form applies to National Power plc, Powergen, Scottish Power, AEA Technology plc, and National Grid Group plc.

The rights attached to the special share are wider in only a few cases where a national 'strategic' interest could be identified. In this case, the consent of the special shareholder is usually required for the voluntary winding up or dissolution of the company, a disposal of the whole or a specified part of the assets of the company or of its subsidiary, and also for other certain provisions.

These restrictions apply to some important privatized companies. In Rolls-Royce plc (operating also in defence), any disposal of a material part of assets of either the group as a whole or its nuclear business (a disposal is material if the net assets disposed are 25 per cent or more of the net asset value or average profits of either the group or its nuclear business). Moreover, the majority of the board must be British. In BAE Systems (aerospace), the government retained the right to appoint a member of the board with voting rights as its representative till May 2002.

For British Energy, any change to the articles of its subsidiaries Nuclear Electric and Scottish Nuclear, the disposal by any means by the company of shares in Nuclear Electric or Scottish Nuclear, and the appointment of the chairman of the board are effective only with the consent of the special shareholder. The company should also remain under national control, and three-quarters of board members and the chairman must be British citizens. For BAA plc (airports utility) the disposal of a designated airport requires prior authorization. For Cable & Wireless (telecommunications) the creation or issue of any shares carrying different voting rights with respect to those attached to the ordinary shares is not effective unless approved by the government.

There are also significant differences in the ways in which these special powers expire. The greater part of English golden shares, in fact, have a limited duration or an expiry date (March 1995 for the twelve Regional Electric Companies), or have been redeemed (Britoil in 1990, Cable & Wireless in 1999, British Telecom in 1997, National Power and British Gas in 2000). As for British Energy, the special share has no expiry date, but it can be redeemed only after September 2006.

Ireland

In Ireland, special powers attributed in Irish privatized companies such as Greencore Group (agriculture) and Irish Life (insurance) are more extensive than the English. The special shareholder's approval is required for any change on ownership limits and for the consolidation or cancellation of the share capital. Prior consent is also required to authorize the sale, transfer, or disposal of more than 20 per cent of the total assets, and to approve indemnities to directors and officers.

There are no time limits for the special powers.

New Zealand

In New Zealand, the government holds special shares called *kiwi shares*. As to Telecom Corporation of New Zealand (telecommunications), the company must obtain consent from the special shareholder for business acquisitions above NZ$10 million. The board of directors has to observe certain principles relating to the provision of telephone services and their prices, which have been established by the holder of the kiwi share. No person may have a relevant interest in 10 per cent or more of the company's voting shares without the prior written approvals of the board and the holder of the kiwi share. The approval of the special shareholder is also required for the acquisition of a 'relevant interest' in more than 49.9 per cent of the voting shares by foreigner investors, also acting in concert.

The privatization of New Zealand Air (the national air carrier) took place through the issue of type A shares reserved for citizens of New Zealand; type B shares reserved for foreign investors; and the kiwi share which, although without voting rights, requires the consent of the kiwi shareholder (the government) for certain important decisions, such as the modification of the company charter, mergers and acquisitions, change of name, or company location.

There is no time limit for the kiwi shares.

France

In France, the content of the French *action spécifique* is particularly diversified. In general, prior approval of the minister is required if persons or entities were to hold more than a certain percentage of the capital or voting rights (10 per cent for Elf Aquitaine, now Total-Fina Elf, Havas, and Thomson-CSF, now Thales). Usually a representative of the French government is appointed to the board of directors acting on behalf of the minister. In some cases he has limited veto power (i.e. for Elf Aquitaine to block the sale of certain strategic assets), while in others he can veto any board resolution (Thomson-CSF, now Thales).

The French government also granted themselves special voting rights by the issue of dual class shares in Total until 1999 when the company merged with the Belgian group Petrofina. 'A' class shares may only be allotted to the French state, public bodies, or persons subject to governmental control, and only with the prior approval of the representative of the government. 'A' shares also have a special voting power at general meetings (total 'A' shares plus 5 per cent of the total voting power of the 'A' class) until the French state or other public bodies retain 25 per cent or more of those shares. Also, 'B' shares owned by the state or public bodies may only be transferred to other entities controlled by the state: only other 'B' shares may be transferred without restrictions.

The privatization decree of 1986 set a maximum duration of five years on the *action spécifique* after which it would be converted into an ordinary share, unless the relevant ministry had given a different indication. The 1993 law did not set a limit in time but gave the government the option of conversion at any moment.

Belgium

In Belgium, an example of multiple restrictions and broad special powers granting the government full control of the company is the *action spécifique* issued for Distrigaz. It affords the special shareholder, through its two representatives in the executive board and in the board of directors, a veto right on any issue. It also requires the consent of the special shareholder for any transaction over 5 per cent of the share capital. Moreover, the special share also gives special voting rights to secure the majority of votes cast in general meetings. No time limit is set for the special powers.

Italy

In Italy, golden shares in Eni, Enel, Telecom Italia, and Finmeccanica have a similar content. Ministry approval is required for a material acquisition of shares representing 3 per cent or more of the share capital, or voting share capital. Voting rights are reduced correspondingly to 3 per cent, but this restriction does not apply to any shareholding held by the Italian state, public entities, or other entities controlled by the state. Authorization is also required for material shareholders' agreements (3 per cent or 5 per cent of the share capital) Furthermore, the ministry appoints one member of the board of directors and one of the board of statutory auditors, in addition to the members appointed in its capacity as shareholder.

The special shareholder may exercise the veto power over major changes such as the dissolution of the company, its transfer, merger or de-merger, the transfer of the head-quarters outside Italy, the change of corporate purposes, or the amendment or modification of any of the special powers.

In the case of Finmeccanica, the special share grants to the government the right to appoint from one board member to a maximum of one-quarter of board members, and extends the veto rights to the sale of a business or line of business, including the transfer of equity participation in subsidiaries or affiliates.

Italy has not imposed any temporal limit on the special powers of the Treasury. For Enel, these are set to be verified after a period of five years (in 2005). As for Telecom Italia, the special powers were to be maintained for a period of three years from privatization, or until the complete liberalization of the telecommunications sector, but they are still valid

Portugal

In Portugal, special powers and constraints stem from the government's possession of special class shares. Portugal Telecom issued multiple class shares outstanding. Type 'A' shares must be held only by either the Portuguese government or by a state majority-owned and controlled entity. 'A' shareholders nominate one-third of the directors, including the chairman, and may veto a number of shareholders' actions, such as the approval of a dividend in excess of 40 per cent of the net income in any year; capital increases, issuance of bonds and other securities; authorization to hold more than 5 per cent of ordinary shares if the acquiring person is a competitor; altering general objectives, strategy, or policies; defining the investment policies, including the authorization of acquisitions and dispositions. Moreover, the company by-laws set a 10 per cent limit of shares ownership.

Spain

In Spain, a regulatory framework for privatized companies operating in 'strategic' sectors of national interest (i.e. Repsol and Endesa in energy, Indra in defence, Telefonica in telecommunications, Iberia in air transports) was introduced by the Spanish privatization law of 1995. According to the system of *autorización administrativa previa*, a prior authorization by the ministry is required for acquisitions over 10 per cent of the capital and for other company acts, such as change of activity, dissolution, spin-off, or fusion. Only for Indra has the Ministry of Defence wider powers involving control of activity related to contracts with the Spanish state. The Spanish governments do not appoint any representative to the board.

The provisions of the 1995 law will expire after a period of five to ten years from the privatization date and cannot be renewed.

Turkey

In Turkey some special powers are so extensive that they involve the government in ordinary management of the company. For example, in the Turkish company Usas Ucaç Servisi the affirmative vote of the representative of the government is required in order to pass a resolution with respect to 'fundamental matters' indicated in the company's statute. The list includes the issuance of additional stock from the company; any merger or sale of assets representing 25 per cent of the total book value, or assets which produce 20 per cent of the net profits; the involuntary termination of more than 5 per cent of the workforce for one year after August 1989 or of more than 10 per cent for each year in the nine years thereafter; the appointment of an outside auditing firm; any increase in the budget for expatriate senior management, experts, or consultants.

Table A3.1. Golden shares around the world

This table presents a list of 'strategic' privatized firms in a sample of developed countries. For each privatized company the residual stake held by the state and the eventual existence of a golden share (Y/N) are reported as of end year 2002.

Sector	Italy	Residual stake (%)	Special powers or restrictions	UK	Residual stake (%)	Special powers or restrictions	Germany	Residual stake (%)	Special powers or restrictions
Oil & gas	ENI	30,33	Y	BP	0	N			
				BRITISH GAS	0	N			
Electricity	ENEL	67,57	Y	BRITISH ENERGY	0	Y	E.ON	4,5	N
				REC	0	N			
				SCOTTISH POWER	0	Y			
				SCOTTISH & SOUTH	0	Y			
				NATIONAL GRID	0	Y			
				NATIONAL POWER	0	N			
				VIRIDIAN GROUP	0	Y			
				POWERGEN	0	N			
Tlc	TELECOM ITALIA	0	Y	BT–BRITISH TELECOM	0	N	DEUTSCHE TELEKOM	59	N
				CABLE & WIRELESS	0	N			
Aerospace & defence	FINMECCANICA	32,45	Y	ROLLS ROYCE	0	Y			
				BRITISH AEROSPACE	0	Y			
Transports	ALITALIA	62,4	Y	BRITISH AIRWAYS	0	Y	LUFTHANSA	41	Y
	AUTOSTRADE	0	N	BAA PLC	0	Y			
	AEROPORTI ROMA	0	N	RAILTRACK GROUP	0	Y			

Table A3.1. (*Cont.*)

Sector	France	Residual stake (%)	Special powers or restrictions	Spain	Residual stake (%)	Special powers or restrictions	Portugal	Residual stake (%)	Special powers or restrictions
Oil & gas									
	TOTALFINA ELF	0	Y	REPSOL YPF	0	Y	PETROGAL	75	N
				GASNATURAL	0	N			
Electricity									
				ENDESA	0	Y	EDP	30,85	Y
				REDESA	28,5	N			
				IBERDROLA	0	N			
Tlc									
	FRANCE TELECOM	42,9	N	TELEFONICA	0	Y	PORTUGAL TELECOM	5	Y
Aerospace & defence									
	THALES	32,6	Y	INDRA SISTEMAS	0	Y			
Transports									
	AIR FRANCE	55,9	Y	IBERIA	0	Y			

Table A3.1. (*Cont.*)

Sector	Austria	Residual stake (%)	Special powers or restrictions	Denmark	Residual stake (%)	Special powers or restrictions	Netherlands	Residual stake (%)	Special powers or restrictions
Oil & gas	OMV AG	54,6	N						
Electricity	VERBUND	51	Y						
	EVN	0	N						
Tlc	TELEKOM AUSTRIA	48	N	TELEDANMARK	51	Y	KPN	34,77	Y
Aerospace & defence									
Transports	AUSTRIAN AIRLINES	75	Y	COPENHAGEN AIRP.	75	Y	KLM AIRLINES	39	Y
	FLUGHAFEN WIEN AG	17,38	N				TNT P.G. NV	36,7	Y

Table A3.1. (Cont.)

Sector	Belgium	Residual stake (%)	Special powers or restrictions	Greece	Residual stake (%)	Special powers or restrictions	Finland	Residual stake (%)	Special powers or restrictions
Oil & gas	DISTRIGAZ	16,6	Y	HELLENIC PETROLEUM	77	Y			
Electricity				NATIONAL ELECTRIC	70	N			
Tlc				OTE	65	Y			
Aerospace & defence									
Transports							FINNAIR	62	Y

Table A3.1. (Cont.)

Sector	Australia	Residual stake (%)	Special powers or restrictions	Canada	Residual stake (%)	Special powers or restrictions	Norway	Residual stake (%)	Special powers or restrictions
Oil & gas				PETROCANADA	18,3	Y	STATOIL	80	N
				TARRAGON OIL & GAS	0	N			
				ALBERTA ENERGY	0	Y			
Electricity				NOVA SCOTIA P.H.	0	Y			
Tlc	TELSTRA CORP.	0	Y	TELUS CORP.	0	Y	TELENOR	79	N
Aerospace & defence							RAUFOSS ASA	50,3	N
Transports	QANTAS AIRWAYS	0	Y	AIR CANADA	0	Y			
				CANADIAN RAILWAYS CO	60	N			

Table A3.1. (Cont.)

Sector	Japan	Residual stake (%)	Special powers or restrictions	New Zealand	Residual stake (%)	Special powers or restrictions
Oil & gas				PETROCORP	64	N
Electricity						
Tlc	NT&T	46	Y	TELECOM CORP	0	Y
Aerospace & defence						
Transports						
	JAPAN AIRLINES	0	N	AIR NEW ZEALAND	0	Y
	EAST JAPAN RAILWAYS	0	N			

Sources: Companies Prospectus, Annual Reports; Institutional Sources (Privatization Agencies, Ministries of Treasury); Thomson Financial–Global Access, Bloomberg; Fondazione Eni Enrico Mattei.

References

Aghion, P., and Bolton, P. (1990). 'Government domestic debt and the risk of a default: a political-economic model of a strategic role of debt', in R. Dornbusch and M. Draghi (eds.), *Public Debt Management: Theory and History*. Cambridge: Cambridge University Press.

Alesina, A., and Drazen, A. (1991). 'Why are stabilizations delayed?' *American Economic Review*, 81: 1170–88.

Amemiya, T. (1985). *Advanced Econometrics*. Oxford: Basil Blackwell.

Ang, J., and Boyer, C. (2000). 'Finance and politics: special interest group influence during the nationalization and privatization of Conrail'. Florida State University, mimeo.

Aron, R. (1982). 'Alternation in government in industrialised countries', *Government and Opposition*, 17: 3–21.

Baer, W., and Birch, M. H. (eds.) (1994). *Privatisation in Latin America*. Westport, Coun.: Praeger.

Bala, J. J. (1995). 'The impacts of privatization on distributional equity in Nigeria', in V. V. Ramanadham (ed.), *Privatization and Equity*. London: Routledge.

Banks, A. S., Day, A. J., and Muller, T. C. (eds.) (1997). *The Political Handbook of the World*. Binghamton: CSA Publications.

Bastos, C., and Abdala, M. A. (1996). *Reform of the Electric Power Sector in Argentina*. World Bank and the Secretary of Argentina.

Beck, T., Demirgüç-Kunt, A., and Levine, R. (1999). 'A new database on financial development and structure', World Bank Policy Research Working Paper n. 2146.

Berle, A., and Means, G. (1932). *The Modern Corporation and Private Property*. New York: Macmillan.

Biais, B., and Perotti, E. C. (2002). 'Machiavellian privatization', *American Economic Review*, 92: 240–58.

Blanchard, O., and Aghion, P. (1996). 'On insider privatisation', *European Economic Review*, 40: 759–66.

Bolton, P. (1995). 'Privatisation and the separation of ownership and control: lessons from the Chinese enterprise reform', *Economics of Transition*, 3: 1–12.

Bortolotti, B., and Pinotti, P. (2003). 'The political economy of privatization', *FEEM Note di Lavoro*, 45: 03.

——, Fantini, M., and Scarpa, C. (2002). 'Why do governments sell privatised companies abroad?', *International Review of Finance*, 3: 131–63.

——, ——, and Siniscalco, D. (2001). 'Privatisation: politics, institutions, and financial markets', *Emerging Market Review*, 2: 109–36.

——, ——, —— (2003). 'Privatisation around the world', *Journal of Public Economics*, 88: 305–32.

——, De Jong, F., Nicodano, G., and Schindele, I. (2002). 'Privatization and stock market liquidity', *FEEM Note di Lavoro*, 105.

Boubakri, N., Cosset, J. C., and Guedhami, O. (2003). 'Post-privatization corporate governance: the role of ownership structure and investor protection', *FEEM Note di Lavoro*, 35.

Boutchkova, M. K., and Megginson, W. L. (2000). 'Privatization and the role of global capital markets', *Financial Management*, 29: 31–76.

Boycko, M., Shleifer, A., and Vishny, R. W. (1994). 'Voucher privatisation', *Journal of Financial Economics*, 35: 249–66.

Boycko, M., Shleifer, A., and Vishny, R. W. (1995). *Privatising Russia*. Cambridge, Mass.: MIT Press.

Braeutigam, R. (1989). 'Optimal policies for natural monopolies', in R. Schmalansee and R. Willig (eds.), *Handbook of Industrial Organization*. Amsterdam: North-Holland.

Branco, F., and Mello, A. (1991). 'A theory of partial sales and underpricing in privatizations', Sloan School of Management, MIT, mimeo.

Brannman, L., Douglass, K., and Weiss, L. (1984). 'Concentration and winning bids in auctions', *Antitrust Bulletin*, 29: 27–31.

Cabello, R., and Shiguiyama, D. (1998). 'Peru's privatization program, 1990–96', in I. W. Lieberman and C. D. Kirkness (eds.), *Privatization and Emerging Equity Markets*, Washington: World Bank and Flemings.

Campbell, J. (1996). 'Understanding risk and return', *Journal of Political Economy*, 104: 298–345.

Castater, N. M. (2002). 'Privatization as a means to societal transformation: an empirical study of privatization in Central and Eastern Europe and the former Soviet Union', *FEEM Note di Lavoro*, 76.

Cavazzuti, F. (1996). *Privatizzazioni imprenditori e mercati*, Bologna: il Mulino.

Chiesa, G., and Nicodano, G. (2003). 'Privatization and financial market development: theoretical issues', *FEEM Note di Lavoro*, 1.

Chiri, S., and Panetta, F. (1994). 'Privatizzare: come? Spunti da una ricognizione comparata dei casi inglese e francese', in *Il mercato della proprietà e del controllo delle imprese: aspetti teorici ed istituzionali, Contributi di Analisi Economica*, Rome: Banca d'Italia.

Clarke T., and Pitelis, C. (eds.) (1993). *The Political Economy of Privatization*. London: Routledge.

Coase, R. (1937). 'The nature of the firm', *Economica*, 4: 386.

Coleman, D. C. (1987). 'Jean-Baptiste Colbert', in J. Eatwell, M. Milgate, and P. Newman (eds.), *The New Palgrave Dictionary of Economics*. London: Macmillan.

Cornelli, F., and Li, D. D., (1997). 'Large shareholders, control benefits and optimal schemes for privatization', *RAND Journal of Economics*, 28: 585–604.

Demirguç-Kunt A., and Levine, R. (1996). 'Stock market development and financial intermediaries: stylised facts', *The World Bank Economic Review*, 10: 291–321.

Dewenter, K., and Malatesta, P. H. (1997). 'Public offerings of state-owned and privately owned enterprises: an international comparison', *Journal of Finance*, 57: 1659–79.

Doidge, C., Karolyi, A. G., and Stultz, R. (2001). 'Why are foreign firms listed in the US worth more?', *NBER* working paper n. 8538.

Dumez, H., and Jeunemaître, A. (1994). 'Privatization in France: 1983–1993', in V. Wright (ed.), *Privatization in Western Europe*, London: Pinter Publishers.

El-Naggar, S. (ed.) (1989). *Privatisation and Structural Adjustment in the Arab Countries*. Washington: IMF.

Esser, J. (1994). 'Germany: "Symbolic privatisations in a social market economy"', in V. Wright (ed.), *Privatization in Western Europe*, London: Pinter Publishers.

Faccio, M., and Lang, L. H. P. (2002). 'The ultimate ownership of Western European corporations', *Journal of Financial Economics*, 65: 365–95.

Faure-Grimaud, A. (2002). 'Using stock price information to regulate firms', *Review of Economic Studies*, 69: 169–90.

Goldstein, M. A., and Gultekin, N. B. (1995). 'Privatization in post-communist economies', Wharton School, University of Pennsylvania, mimeo.

Graham, C., and Prosser, T. (1991). *Privatizing Public Enterprises*, Oxford: Clarendon Press.

Green, R., and Newbery, D. (1998). 'The electricity industry in England and Wales', in D. Helm and T. Jenkinson (eds.), *Competition in Regulated Industries*. Oxford: Oxford University Press.

Grossman, S. (1976). 'On the efficiency of competitive stock markets where traders have diverse information', *Journal of Finance*, 31: 573–85.

—, and Hart, O. (1980). 'Disclosure laws and take-over bids', *Bell Journal of Economics*, 11: 42–64.

—, — (1986). 'The costs and benefits of ownership: a theory of vertical and lateral integration', *Journal of Political Economy*, 94: 691–719.

Guislain, P. (1997). *The Privatization Challenge*. Washington: World Bank.

Gupta, N. (2002). 'Partial privatization and firm performance', *FEEM Note di Lavoro*, 110.

Hart, O., and Moore, J. (1988). 'Incomplete contracts and renegotiations', *Econometrica*, 56: 755.

—, Shleifer, A., and Vishny, R. W. (1997). 'The proper scope of government: theory and an application to prisons', *Quarterly Journal of Economics*, 112: 1127–61.

Hayek, F. A. (1994). *The Road to Serfdom*. Chicago: University of Chicago Press.

Helm, D., and Jenkinson, T. (1998). 'Introducing competition into regulated industries', in D. Helm and T. Jenkinson (eds.), *Competition in Regulated Industries*. Oxford: Oxford University Press.

Hertig, G. (2000). 'Western Europe corporate dilemma', in T. Baums, K. J. Hopt, and N. Horn (eds.), *Corporations, Capital Markets, and Business in the Law*. Kluwer Law International.

Hölmstrom, B., and Tirole, J. (1993). 'Market liquidity and performance monitoring', *Journal of Political Economy*, 101: 678–709.

Huber, J., and Inglehart, R. (1995). 'Expert interpretations of party space and party locations in 42 societies', *Party Politics*, 1: 73–111.

Jenkinson, T., and Ljungqvist, A. P. (2000). *Going Public*. Oxford: Oxford University Press.

Jensen, M. C., and Meckling, W. R. (1976). 'Theory of the firm: managerial behaviour, agency costs, and ownership structure', *Journal of Financial Economics*, 3: 305–60.

Jones, S., Megginson, W. L., Nash, R., and Netter, J. (1999). 'Share issue privatizations as financial means to political and economic ends', *Journal of Financial Economics*, 53: 217–53.

Kay, J. A., Mayer, C., and Thompson D. J. (eds.) (1986). *Privatization and Regulation: the UK Experience*. Oxford: Clarendon Press.

Klein, B., Crawford, R. G., and Alchian, A. A. (1978). 'Vertical integration, appropriable rents, and the competitive contracting process', *Journal of Law and Economics*, 21: 297.

La Porta, R., López-de-Silanes, F., and Shleifer, A. (2002). 'Government ownership of commercial banks', *Journal of Finance*, 57: 265–302.

—, —, —, and Vishny, R. W. (1997). 'Legal determinants of external finance', *Journal of Finance*, 52: 1131–50.

—, —, —, — (1998). 'Law and finance', *Journal of Political Economy*, 106: 1113–55.

La Porta, R., López-de-Silanes, F., Shleifer, A., and Vishny, R. W. (1999a). 'Corporate ownership around the world', *Journal of Finance*, 54: 471–518.

—, —, —, — (1999b). 'The quality of government', *Journal of Law, Economics, and Organizations*, 15: 222–79.

Laakso, M., and Taagepera, R. (1979). 'Effective number of parties: a measure with application to West Europe', *Comparative Political Studies*, 12: 3–27.

Laffont, J. J., and Meleu, M. (1997). 'A positive theory of privatisation in sub-Saharan Africa', Toulouse University, mimeo.

Laffont, J. J., and Tirole, J. (1991). 'Privatization and incentives', *Journal of Law, Economics and Organization*, 7: 84–105.

Larroulet, C. (1995). 'The impacts of privatization on distributional equity: the Chilean case, 1985–9', in V. V. Ramanadham (ed.), *Privatization and Equity*. London and New York: Routledge.

—, — (1993). *The Theory of Procurement and Regulation*. Cambridge, Mass.: MIT Press.

Levine, R. (1997). 'Financial development and economic growth: views and agenda', *Journal of Economic Literature*, 35: 688–726.

—, and Zervos, S. (1998). 'Stock markets, banks, and economic growth', *American Economic Review*, 88: 537–58.

Lewington, I. (1997). 'Utility regulation', *Privatisation International*. London: Privatisation International Ltd.

Li, W. (1997). 'The impact of economic reform on the performance of Chinese state enterprises, 1980–1989', *Journal of Political Economy*, 105: 1080–106.

Lieberman, I. W., and Fergusson, R. (1998). 'Overview of privatization and emerging equity markets', in I. W. Lieberman and C. D. Kirkness (eds.), *Privatization and Emerging Equity Markets*. Washington: World Bank and Flemings.

Lijphart, A. (1999). *Patterns of Democracy*. New Haven and London: Yale University Press.

Ljungqvist, A. P., Jenkinson, T., and Wilhelm, W. J. Jr (2000). 'Has the introduction of bookbuilding increased the efficiency of international IPOs?', Working paper, Stern School of Business, New York.

López-de-Silanes, F. (1997). 'Determinants of privatization prices', *Quarterly Journal of Economics*, 112: 965–1025.

—, Shleifer, A., and Vishny, R. (1997). 'Privatization in the United States', *The RAND Journal of Economics*, 28: 447–71.

Macchiati, A. (1996). *Privatizzazioni, fra economia e politica*. Rome: Donzelli.

Manzetti, L. (1997). 'Privatization and regulation: lessons from Argentina and Chile', *The North-South Agenda Papers*, 24.

Megginson, W. L., and Netter, J. (2001). 'From state to market: a survey of empirical studies on privatization', *Journal of Economic Literature*, 39: 321–89.

—, Nash, R. C., and van Randenborgh, M. (1994). 'The financial and operating performance of newly privatised firms: an international empirical analysis', *Journal of Finance*, 49: 403–52.

—, —, Netter, J. M., and Poulsen, A. B. (2000). 'The choice between private and public markets: evidence from privatizations', Working paper, Athens, University of Georgia.

Milgrom, P. (1987). 'Auction theory', in T. Bewley (ed.), *Advances in Economic Theory*, Cambridge, Mass.: Cambridge University Press.

—, and Roberts, J. (1982). 'Predation, reputation, and entry deterrence', *Journal of Economic Theory*, 27: 280–312.

—, and Weber, R. (1982). 'A theory of auctions and competitive bidding', *Econometrica*, 50: 1081.

Ministero del Tesoro (1992). *Libro verde delle partecipazioni dello Stato*. Rome: Poligrafico dello Stato.

Mustafa, M. A., and Fink, C. (1998). 'Tapping international equity markets through depositary receits: lessons from the telecoms sector', *Private Sector*, 3: 49–52.

O'Hara, M. (1995). *Market Microstructure Theory*. Cambridge, Mass.: Basil Blackwell.

Pagano, M. (1993). 'The flotation of companies and the stock market: a co-ordination failure model', *European Economic Review*, 37: 1101–25.

Perotti, E. (1995). 'Credible privatization', *American Economic Review*, 85: 847–59.

—, and Guney, S. E. (1993). 'Successful privatization plans: enhanced credibility through timing and pricing of sales', *Financial Management*, 22: 84–98.

—, and Laeven, L. (2002). 'Confidence building in emerging stock markets', *FEEM Note di Lavoro*, 101.

—, and Van Oijen, P. (2001). 'Privatization, political risk, and stock market development in emerging economies', *Journal of International Money and Finance*, 20: 43–69.

Persson, T., and Tabellini, G. (2000). *Political Economics: Explaining Economic Policy*. Cambridge, Mass.: MIT Press.

—, — (2001). 'Political institutions and policy outcomes: what are the stylized facts', Università Bocconi, mimeo.

Petrazzini, B. (1996). 'Telephone privatization in a hurry', in R. Ramamurti (ed.), *Privatizing Monopolies: Lessons from the Telecommunications and Transport Sectors in Latin America*. Baltimore: Johns Hopkins University Press.

Ramamurti, R. (ed.) (1996). *Privatising Monopolies: Lessons from the Telecommunications and Transport Sectors in Latin America*. Baltimore: Johns Hopkins University Press.

Roland, G., and Verdier, T. (1994). 'Privatization in Eastern Europe: irreversibility and critical mass effects', *Journal of Public Economics*, 54: 161–83.

Rovinescu, C., and Thieffry, G. (1996). 'Cross-border marketing', in F. Oditah (ed.), *The Future for the Global Securities Market*. Oxford: Clarendon Press.

Sachs, J. D. (1992). 'Privatization in Russia: some lessons from Eastern Europe', *American Economic Review*, 82: 43–8.

Sappington, D., and Stiglitz, J. (1987). 'Privatization, information and incentives', *Journal of Policy Analysis and Management*, 6: 567–82.

Schelling, T. (1960). *The Strategy of Conflict*. Cambridge, Mass.: Harvard University Press.

Schmidt, K. (1996). 'Incomplete contracts and privatization', *European Economic Review*, 40: 569–79.

— (2000). 'The political economy of mass privatization and the risk of expropriation', *European Economic Review*, 44: 393–421.

—, and Schnitzer, K. M. (1997). 'Methods of privatization: auctions, bargaining and giveaways', Center for Economic Policy Research Discussion Paper No. 1441.

Shafer, J. R. (2000). *Privatisation International Yearbook*, Salomon Smith Barney.

Shafik, N. (1995). 'Making a market: mass privatisation in the Czech and Slovak republics', *World Development*, 23: 1143–56.

Shapiro, C., and Willig, R. D. (1990). 'Economic rationales for the scope of privatization', in E. N. Suleiman and J. Waterbury (eds.), *The Political Economy of Public Sector Reform and Privatization*. Boulder, Colo. and London: Westview Press.

References

Sheshinski, E., and López-Calva, L. F. (2000). 'Privatization and its benefits: theory, evidence, and challenges', in K. Basu, P. Nayak, and R. Ray (eds.), *Markets and Governments*. New Delhi: Oxford University Press.

Shirley, M. M., and Walsh, P. (2000). 'Public versus private ownership: the current state of the debate', *World Bank Policy Research Working Paper no. 2420*.

Shleifer, A. (1998). 'State versus private ownership', *Journal of Economic Perspectives*, 12: 133–50.

Shleifer, A., and Vishny, R. (1994). 'Politicians and firms', *Quarterly Journal of Economics*, 109: 995–1025.

Siglienti, S. (1996). *Una privatizzazione molto privata*. Milan: Mondadori.

Smith, A. [1776]. In R. H. Campbell and A. S. Skinner (eds.), *An Inquiry into the Nature and Causes of the Wealth of Nations*. Oxford: Clarendon Press.

Spiller, P. T. (1995). 'Regulatory commitment and utilities' privatisation: implications for future comparative research', in J. Banks and E. Hanushek (eds.), *Modern Political Economy*. Cambridge: Cambridge University Press, pp. 63–79.

Spinnewyn, H. (2000). *Les partecipations publiques dans le secteur marchand en Belgique*. Bureau Fédéral du Plan.

Stiglitz, J. (2002). *Globalization and its Discontents*. New York: Norton.

Subrahmanyam, A., and Titman, S. (1999). 'The going public decision and the development of financial markets', *Journal of Finance*, 54: 1045–82.

Tesche, J., and Tohamy, S. (1994). 'A note on economic liberalisation and privatisation in Hungary and Egypt', *Comparative Economic Studies*, 36: 51–72.

Vickers, J., and Yarrow, G. (1988). *Privatization: an Economic Analysis*. Cambridge, Mass.: MIT Press.

Vickrey, W. (1961). 'Counter speculation, auctions, and competitive sealed tenders', *Journal of Finance*, 16: 8–37.

Wallsten, S. (2001). 'An econometric analysis of Telecom competition, privatization, and regulation in Africa and Latin America', *Journal of Industrial Economics*, 49: 1–20.

Williamson, O. (1985). *The Economic Institutions of Capitalism*. New York: Free Press.

Wint, A. G. (1996). 'Pioneering telephone privatisation: Jamaica', in R. Ramamurti (ed.), *Privatising Monopolies: Lessons from the Telecommunications and Transport Sectors in Latin America*. Baltimore: Johns Hopkins University Press.

World Bank (1995). *Bureaucrats in Business: the Economics and Politics of Government Ownership*. New York: Oxford University Press.

World Bank (2002). *World Development Indicators*, CD-Rom.

Wright V. (ed.) (1994). *Privatisation in Western Europe*. London: Pinter Publishers.

Yergin, D., and Stanislaw, J. (1998). *The Commanding Heights: the Battle Between Government and the Marketplace that is Remarking the Modern World*. New York: Simon & Schuster.

Zhang, Y., Parker, D., and Kirkpatrick, C. (2002). 'Electricity sector reform in developing countries: an econometric assessment of the effects of privatisation, competition and regulation', University of Manchester, mimeo.

Index

Abffidala, M. A. 109
absolutist state 42
accumulation of capital in infrastructures 42
Adanauer government 1, 68
AEA Technology plc 135
aerospace 96
Africa 31
    privatization 46
Aghion, P. 14
Alberta Energy 94
Alesina, A. 53
Alitalia 46, 98
Amemiya, T. 54
American Depository Receipts (ADR) 133
Amihud index 47, 72
Ang, J. 29
Argentina 30, 44, 98, 106, 111, 128
    1992 privatization law 109
    electricity sector, privatization of 104
    utilities 30
        case of 103–5
Aron, R. 130
Asia 21–2, 35–6, 42
    distribution of revenue in 102
    percentage of revenue for the sale of
        utilities 98–9
    process of privatization 35–6
Atlantic Telenetwork 33
auction
    design, optimal 17
    format 16
    IPV 16
    with reverse (not reverse) price 16
    theory 117
Australia 37, 44, 50, 106, 109, 111, 128, 143
Austria 56, 71, 106, 108, 110–11, 129, 141
Autostrade Spa 46
AyE 109

Baer, W. 30
Bahrain 34
Bala, J. J. 69
Balladur, E. 48
Banca Commerciale Italiana 46
Banco del Centro 30
Banco International 30
bank-dominated financial systems 81

banks 37, 121, 126–7
Banoro 30
Bastos, C. 109
Beck, T. 124
Belgacom 52
Belgium 25, 52, 94, 108, 128, 142
    golden shares 137
Benin, constitution of 50
Berle, A. 88
Biais, B. 14, 16, 60
bid-ask spread 47
Birch, M. H. 30
Blanchard, O. 145
Bolivia 50
Bolton, P. 36
book-building 133
Bortolotti, B. 53, 61–2, 68, 72
Boubakri, N. 86
Boutchkova, M. K. 47, 70
Boycko, M. 40–1, 79
Boyer, C. 29
BPL Cellular Holdings 134
Braeutigam, R. 110
Branco, F. 146
Brannman, L. 134
Brazil 30, 46, 106, 128
    constitution 50
Britain see United Kingdom
British Airport Authority (BAA) 24, 135
British Airways 24
British Election Survey 61
British Energy 91, 135–6
British Gas 24, 31, 101, 136
British Petroleum (BP) 24, 89, 98, 101
British Telecom 24, 60, 136
budgetary adjustment 45
'Build-Own-Operate' (BOO) schemes 132
Burkina Faso 33

Cabello, R. 69
Cable & Wireless 135–6
Campbell, J. 130–1
Canada 29, 71, 107, 128, 143
Canadian National Airways 29
capital
    accumulation in infrastructures 42
    markets 39

capital (*cont.*)
  public or private 59
capital-intensive industries 42
capitalization and trading value of privatized
  companies 73–7
Caribbean 28–30, 37, 103
Castater, N. M. 146
categories of privatized firms 84
Cavazzuti, F. 46
Central and Eastern European
  Countries (CEECs) 21
  and the former Soviet Union 38–40
  distribution of revenue in 101
Central Electricity Generating Board
  (CEGB) 109
CGER 52
Chemical Bank 31
Chiesa, G. 47
Chile 1, 69, 107, 109, 111, 128
China 4, 35
China Telecom 35
Chirac 48, 68
Chiri, S. 67
choice of privatization methods 16–19, 21
Clarke, T. 60, 70
classification of shares 36
Coase, R. 116
Coase theorem application to neutrality result 9
cohabitation 130
Colbert, Jean-Baptiste 42
Colbertism 42
Coleman, D. C. 42
Colombia 107, 128
commitment to market oriented policies 68
  the structure of the offer 65–8
Committee on Foreign Investment in the United
  States (CFIUS) 90
common law
  countries 50, 128
  legal origin 5
Compagnie Générale d'Electricité (CGE) 48, 66
comparative political science 53
competitive equilibrium 6
confidence building 18, 66
Conrail 29
Conservative governments 48
conservative party 61
conservatives, privatization backed by
  in Argentina 48
  in France 48
consistency of privatization policy 67
Consolidated Rail Corp 29
constitutions 50

construction 23
  finance 23
  services 23
  transport 23
  utilities 23
Continental Europe 25–7
contracting out 11–12
  in the US 28
control rights
  separation of ownership rights from 8, 88
  separation of property rights from 88
coordination failure among firms and
  investors 19
Cornelli, F. 17
corporate finance literature 88
corporate governance 50
  in utilities 118
corporatized firm 8
Cosset, J. C. 86
costs
  reduction 12
  and benefits of privatization 12
country risk 68
Crawford, R. G. 147
credibility 17–18, 65–8, 81
  deficit 67
  international allocation of shares 67
  over time 66
Credit Suisse 31
creditor protection 51
critical mass of privatizations 13
Croatia 38
crony capitalism 40
cross-listing procedures 132–4
Czechoslovakia 38, 40
  system of vouchers 40

De Jong, F. 72
defence 96
Demirguç-Kunt, A. 69, 124
denationalizaiton 1
  of IRI 25
Denmark 27, 49, 109, 111, 129, 141
  companies 94
Deahene, Prime Minister 52
Depository Receipt (DR) Programme 133
Derksen, W. 121
determinants of privatization 41, 54, 58
Deutsche Telekom 46
developed economies 70
  golden shares mechanisms 90
  value of privatized assets in 44

Dewenter, K. 69
Dexia 52
disproportionality index *see* Gallagher index
Distrigaz 52
diversification 47
diversified mass privatization 14
divestiture 66
　ideological rationale for 70
　of minority holdings 80
　of monopolies 98
　of ownership complete 84
　programme, designing 78
Doidge, C. 132
domestic financial market development 69
　effect of privatization on 71
Douglass, K. 134
Drazen, A. 53
Dresdner Bank 31
Dumez, H. 68

East Japan Railroads 35
Eastern European Countries (CEEC)
　and the former Soviet Union
　privatization in 39–40
economic development 54
　role of 44
　theory of the stages of 42
economic factors, long-term 58
economic and financial variables 124–5
economic theory of privatization 5
Ecuador 44, 128
Edmonton Telephones 29
Effective Number of Parties Index
　(ENP) 53
Egypt 34, 128
electoral success for liberal–conservative
　coalitions 60
Electoral Web Sites 121
Electrabel 108
electricity 96
　generation
　　and distribution, aspects of
　　　regulation in 110
　　privatization in 105–8, 115
　sector
　　privatization in 114
　　regulation 108–10, 112
　wholesale market for 111
Electrolima 109
Electroperu 109
EL-EX in Finland 111
Elf Aquitaine *see* Total-Fina Elf
El-Naggar, S. 33

empirical analyses, data and
　methodology 121–31
Endesa 94, 138
Enel 25, 46, 137
energy, telecom, and utility industries 72
England and Wales 107, 111
　blueprint for liberalization and restructuring
　　in electricity sector 109
Eni 98, 137
Entel 103–4
equity culture 78
　development of 70
Estonia 38
Europe 42, 50
European Directive for Internal Electricity
　Market 111
European privatization, goals of 27
expropriation 14
　of private investment 68
external social benefits 7

Faccio, M. 84–5
failed privatization attempts 1
Fantini, M. 61–2, 68
Faure-Grimaud, A. 47
Federal Republic of Germany 1
Fergusson, R. 69
financial market
　developed 80
　development 18, 68–70
　　role of 54
　impact of privatization on 72
　liquidity 18
　role of 46–8
Fink, C. 133–4
Finland 27, 90, 107, 111, 129, 142
Finmeccanica 91, 137
first tranche 83
fiscal crises, history of 28
fiscal deficits 61
fiscal distress 54
foreign capital 39
foreigners
　participation of 39
　opening of capital to 21
foreign exchange, liquid 65
former Soviet Union 21, 38–40
　method of sale 39
　percentage of revenue for the sale
　　of utilities 98–9
　see also Central and Eastern European
　　Countries (CEECs)

France 25, 44–5, 66, 71, 83, 96, 128–9, 140
  1946 Constitution 50
  EdF in 108
  golden shares 136
  privatization 48, 67, 98
France Telecom 33, 98
French Civil Law 128
  countries 49–50
full privatization
  in civil law countries 81
  partial privatization 13
fundamental privatization theorem 7

Gallagher index 53
Gazprom 39
GDP 55, 57
  comparison of revenue average values to 44
  SOE investment as proportion of 49
General Accepted Accounting Principles
    (GAAP) 133
German civil law 80
  countries 49
  tradition 51, 56
German Scandinavian Law 129
Germany 44, 56, 68, 71, 107, 109, 111, 129, 139
  legal origin 81
  privatization process 46
Global Depository Receipts (GDR) 133
global economic recovery 120
global equity market placement, privatization
    through a 68
global privatization process 35
golden shares 79, 137
  around the world 135–44
  definition 89
  institutional information about 90
  intensity of 92–3
  mechanisms 21
  negative relationship between extent of
      privatization and use of 96
  in privatized companies, application of 90
  and special rights 88–91
  in strategic sectors
    defining national interests 89
    measuring 91–6
Goldstein, M. A. 39
governments
  as benevolent dictator 10
  budget constraints 45–6, 58
  control in strategic vs. non-strategic
      sectors 34
  credibility 68
  design of privatization 59

preferences 12, 18
  relinquishment of control 84
Graham, C. 50
Great Britain *see* United Kingdom
Great Bull Market of the 1990s 47
Greece 25, 128, 142
  PPC in 108
Greencore Group 136
Green, R. 109
Grossman, S. 9, 88
Guedhami, O. 86
Guislain, P. 45, 134
Gultekin, N. B. 39
Guney, S. E. 67
Gupta, N. 83

Hart, O. 9, 11, 88, 101, 116
Havas 136
Hayek, F. A. 5
Helm, D. 102
Herfindal concentration
    index 53
Hertig, G. 82
Hidronor 109
Highway 407 29
Holland 25, 128
Hölmstrom, B. 47
Hong Kong 36, 128
hostile take-overs 89
hot markets 47, 55, 58
Howe, Geoffrey 23
Huber 127
Hungary 38–40

Iberia 94
income inequality 62
incomplete contracts approach 9–12
independent private values (IPV) 16
India 4, 44, 128
  cellular phone sector 134
  sales in 134
individual investors 68
Indonesia 50, 128
Indostat 35
Indra 138
industrial sectors 130
information
  about profitability of firm 7
  aggregation 47
  difference between state-owned and
      private firms 7
  problems 11
innovation 12

IPOs (initial public offerings),
  number of 19
institutional aspects of regulation 111
institutional credibility and commitment
  in policy making 66
institutional systems
  characterization of executive 53
  ideal models, majoritarian and
    consensus 53
insurance 37
international investment, attracting in
  SOEs of strategic importance 32
international markets, flotation
  on efficient 36
international offering 62
international profile of sale 59
international share issue privatization
  (ISIP) 61
  probability of 63–5
investigation of privatization,
  results of 3–4
investor protection 50, 80
  importing 132–4
investors' diversification opportunities,
  improved 18
Ireland 1, 25, 110, 128
  electricity supply board in 108
  golden shares 136
Irish Life 136
irrelevance result 7
Iscor 32
Israel 34, 128
Italy 25, 44–5, 71, 83, 94, 128, 139
  Amato and Ciampi governments 46
  ENEL in 108
  Genco 25
  golden shares 137
  privatization process 46, 98
  programme for the Stability Pact 68
Ivory Coast 33

Jamaica 29
Japan 35–6, 44, 49, 56, 71, 129, 144
  telecommunications monopoly 47
Japan Telecom *see* Nippon Telegraph
    and Telephone (NTT)
Jenkinson, T. 59–60, 102
Jensen, M. C. 47, 88
Jeunemaître, A. 68
Jones, S. 61–2, 67
Jordan 44, 128
Jospin, L. 48
Juppé, A. 48

Karolyi, A. G. 132
Kay, J. A. 24
Kenya 32, 44, 128
Kenya Airways 33
Kirkpatrick, C. 111
kiwi share *see* New Zealand
Klein, B. 101
KLM 33
Korea Telecom 35
Kuwait Investment Office (KIO) 89

La Porta, R. 41, 49–51, 64, 121, 127, 129
Laakso, M. 53
Laeven, L. 19, 66, 71
Laffont, J. J. 11, 110
Lang, I. H. P. 84–5
Laroullet 69
Latin America 21–2, 30–1, 42
  distribution of revenue in 100
  percentage of revenue for sale of
    utilities 98–9
  privatization in 31, 46
Latvia 38
Lebanon 34
legal origins of state owned enterprise
  sectors 49
legal traditions 50, 58
legislative control over public budgets 28
less developed countries (LDCs) 44
  privatizations in 70
Levine, R. 46–7, 69, 124
Lewington, I. 105, 129
liberalization 102
Li, D. D. 17
Lieberman, I. W. 69
Lijphart, A. 53, 126–7
limited privatizations 44
liquidity 46
  measures of 47
Li, W. 36
Ljungqvist, A. P. 59–60
London Stock Exchange (LSE) 132–3
López-Calva, I. F. 6, 83, 132
López-de-Silanes, F. 28, 41, 49–51, 134
low liquidity-high risk premium
    equilibrium 18
Lukoil 39

Maastricht convergence criteria 52
Maastricht Treaty, deficit and debt targets 46
Macchiati, A. 46
Magnox Electric PLC 24
majoritarian political systems 52, 54

Malatesta, P. H. 69
Malaysia 50, 128
managers 7, 47
Manzetti, L. 103, 105
market
  capitalization 47
    and liquidity 81
    role in privatization 55
  regulation 110–13
  share 53
  structure and regulation on
    privatization, effect of 102
Maroc Telecom 34
Martens, Prime Minister 52
mass privatization 40
  process in Russia 40
Mayer, C. 24
Means, G. 88
Meckling, W. R. 47, 88
Megginson, W. L. 24, 35, 47, 61–2, 67,
  69–70
Meleu, M. 148
Middle East and North Africa (MENA) 38
  distribution of revenue in 101
  privatization process in 33
Menem, Carlos 48, 103
Metrogas 31
Mexico 30, 45, 128
  constitution 50
Middle East 33–4, 42
  percentage of revenue for sale of
    utilities 98–9
  privatization 46
Milgrom, P. 66, 117, 134
minority stakes, sale of 67
Mitterand 66
monopoly
  privatizing 98
  firm producing a public good 10
  rights 50
Moore, J. 101, 116
Morocco 34, 50
Mosenergo 39
Multibanco Comermex 30
multiple equilibria 13
Mustafa, M. A. 133–4

NASDAQ 132
Nash, R. C. 24, 61–2, 67, 69–70
national airports 49
National Grid Group plc 109, 135
national industrial policy objectives 89

nationalization decree 66
National Power 109, 135–6
National Union of Mineworkers 52
Netherlands the 27, 111, 141
Netter, J. M. 35, 61–2, 67, 69–70
neutrality theorems 6–9
New York stock exchange (NYSE) 36, 132
New Zealand 44, 50, 71, 107, 111, 128, 144
  kiwi shares 37, 136
  privatizations 37
  telecommunications 37
New Zealand Air 136
Newbery, D. 109
Nicodano, G. 47, 72
Nigeria 32, 44, 83, 128
Nigerian Government Southern
  Oilfields 32
Nippon Telegraph and Telephone (NTT) 35–6
  privatization of 47
Nordpool 111
North Africa 33–4, 42
  percentage of revenue for sale of
    utilities 98–9
North America 37
  and the Caribbean 28–30
    distribution of revenue in 103
Northern Ireland 107
Norway 71, 129, 143
Nuclear Electric 135

Oceania 37, 42
  distribution of revenue in 100
  percentage of revenue for the sale of
    utilities 98–9
  privatization in 37
OECD economies 56, 58, 71, 84, 91
O'Hara, M. 47
opportunity cost 45
optimal number of privatizations 13
optimal regulation under asymmetric
  information 11
outsourcing of public services to private
  operators 28
ownership
  difference between public and private 7
  in privatized companies, ultimate 84–5
  structures
    in developing economies 86
    in privatized firms 84

Pagano, M. 19, 47
Pakistan 107, 128–9
Panetta, F. 67

Paribas 48, 66
Paris stock market, capitalization of 68
Parker, D. 111
parliamentary approval of privatization law 50
parliamentary share 53
partial privatization 80–3
partial sales 83
  explaining 82
parties' 'blackmail' potential 53
PARTISAN (political orientation of
    government) index 56, 58
Péchiney 48, 66
performance of public and private firms 8
Perotti, E. C. 14, 16–119, 60, 66–7, 71
Persson, T. 66, 126, 129
Peru 108, 128–9
  1992 legislative reform 109
  CPT 31
  Entel-Peru 31
  new stock exchange law reform
      of the pension system 69
  privatization programme in 69
Petrazzini, B. 104
Petro-Canada 29
Petrofina 137
Philippines the 110, 128
Pinotti, P. 53
Pitelis, C. 60, 70
Poland 38
policy
  reversals, incentives to 13
  risk, reduction of 18
political aspects of privatization
  partisan model à la Aghion and
      Bolton 14
political competition 83
political economics of privatization 12–16
  consequences of 70–8
political institutions 51–3, 58
political majorities 48–9
political orientation 58
  of privatization governments, methodology
      of identifying 49
political preferences, role in explaining
    privatization methods 62
political variables 121, 126–7
political-institutional index for established
    democracies 53
popular capitalism 60–1
  development of 15
  fostering 65
portfolio diversification 47

Portugal 25, 71, 96, 108, 111, 128, 140
  constitution 50
  golden shares 138
  national telecommunication monopoly 94
Portugal Telecom 138
Poulsen, A. B. 69–70
Powerfin 108
PowerGen 24, 109, 135
pre-privatization policy announcements 66
price formation mechanism 111
pricing strategy, importance of 134
private benefits of control 7
private ownership
  post-privatization 86
  public control 79
privately owned companies 86
private-ownership–public-control pattern 120
privatization 9
  across countries 43–4
  around the world (1977–2001) 2, 21
    ranking 22
    revenue by sectors 23
  and economic development 42–5
  large-scale programme 42
  methods, choice of 16–19, 21
  optimal number of 13
  policy
    failures in Asia, Russia and Latin
        America 4
    rationale for 1
  on public equity markets 62
  revenue/GDP
    around the world 55
    OECD countries 57
  success in terms of proceeds 99
  sustained process 18
  variables 121–3
  waves 55
    associated with economic growth and bull
        stock markets 119
  as a way of attracting foreign capital 31
privatized companies
  capitalization and trading value
      of 73–7
  categories of 84
  control in strategic sectors 97
private sales (PS) 22
  privatizations through 81
property rights
  separation from control rights 88
proportional systems 52
Prosser, T. 50
public equity markets 22

public finance
 beneficial effects of privatization on 45
 role in SOE divestiture 54
public monopoly-turns-into-private monopoly
   argument 118
public offering (PO) 22, 81
 privatizations through 81
 of shares 18

Qualified Institutional Buyers, (QIB) 133
quality of privatization process 117
quantity of state assets sold 118

Raffarin, J. P. 48
Railtrack 24, 66, 94
railway companies 33
Ramamurti, R. 30
Rasmussen 49
Regional Electricity Boards 109
Regional Electricity Companies (RECs) 109, 136
regulation
 and divestiture of monopolies 98
 in infrastructure privatization 110
 review of 14
re-nationalization 13–15
 political costs of 66
 provisions of 66
Repsol 138
reputational mechanism 12
residual average stake and golden
   shares 95
revenues
 and efficiency 16
 equivalence theorem 17
 generation 65
 maximization 70
 non-recurring nature of 45
Rhône Poulenc 48, 66
right wing governments 54, 60, 62
 privatization programmes by 15
Roberts, J. 66
Roland, G. 12–13, 15
Rolls Royce 24, 60, 135
Romania 38
Rovinescu, C. 133
RPI-X or rate of return regulation 111
Russia 3
 decentralized system of local level
   auctions 40
 energy giants 39

Sabena 52
Sachs, J. D. 38

Saint Gobain 48, 66
Salomon Smith Barney 68
Sappington, D. 7
Scandinavia 111
Scarpa, C. 62, 68
Schelling, T. 66
Schindele, I. 72
Schmidt, K. 10–11, 13, 17, 65, 117–18
Schnitzer, K. M. 17, 117
Scotland 108–9
Scottish Nuclear 135
Scottish Power 105, 135
SEC regulations 133
sectors 90
 agriculture 23, 38
 construction 23
 credit 38
 defence 90
 energy 23
 finance 38
 industry 23, 38
 oil and gas 90
 telecommunications 90
 utilities 38, 90
SEGBA 109
Senegal 50
SET (Congo) 33
Shafer, J. R. 149
Shafik, N. 40
Shapiro, C. 7, 10–11
share issue privatizations (SIPs) 60, 72, 90
shares
 'A' class 137
 'B' class 137
 ownership, widening 60–5
 types of 138
 see also golden shares; underpricing
shareholders, inflation in number in
   privatized firms 70
Sheshinski, E. 6, 83, 132
Shiguiyama, D. 69
Shirley, M. M. 6
Shleifer, A. 5, 11–12, 28, 38, 40–1,
   49–51, 79, 88
Shleifer and Vishny's model 8–9
Siglienti, S. 46
Singapore 128
Siniscalco, D. 61
Sirti 46, 98
Smith, Adam 1–2, 45, 48, 120
Socfinal 33
social ownership 61

social welfare 7
Societé des Caoutchous de Grand Béreby
    of the Ivory Coast 32
Societé Nationale d'Investissement
    (SNI) 52
SOEs (state-owned enterprises) 1, 138
    cash flow rights in 45
    investment as proportion of GDP 49
        international 32
    legal origins of 49
    operational performance of 9
    in poorly regulated environments 120
    shareholdings in privatized 84
    value-added 49
Sotelgui (Guineau) 33
South Africa 32, 128
South Korea 56, 129
sovereign debt 54
    and deficits, reduction of 45
Spain 25, 27, 71, 94, 108-9, 111,
    128, 140
    golden shares 138
special debt amortization funds 45
Spiller, P. T. 99
Spinnewyn, H. 52
Sri Lanka 44, 128
Stanislaw, J. 5
state ownership dynamics in privatized
    firms 83-8
'state-owned' firms 84, 86
Stet-France Telecom alliance 104
Stiglitz, J. 7
stock market
    development 81
    liquidity 47, 69, 80
        in OECD countries 72
strategic partnership with foreign
    operators 119
strategic sectors
    control of privatized firms 97
    definition 91
    of OECD countries 94
    of SOEs 32
Stultz, R. 132
Subrahmanyam, A. 19
sub-Saharan Africa 32-3, 37, 42
    distribution of revenue in 102
    privatization in 33
subsidies 45
Suez 48, 66
Sweden 25, 71, 111, 129
Switzerland 27, 44, 56, 129

Taagepera, R. 53
Tabellini, G. 66, 126, 129
Taiwan 56, 129
Telcom (Ivory Coast) 33
Telecom Corporation of New Zealand 136
Telecom Italia 45, 98, 137
Telecom Malaysia 33
Telecommunication of Jamaica 29
telecommunications 27, 38, 96
Telefonica de Espana 30-1, 94, 104, 138
Telefonica Larga Distancia di Porto Rico 30
telephone companies in South Africa and
    Ghana 33
Telkom 32
Telstra 94
Tesche, J. 34
Thailand 108, 110, 128
Thatcher, Margaret 1-2, 23, 42, 61, 98
    government privatization programme 60, 67
Thieffry, G. 133
Third Party Access (TPA) 111
Thompson, D. J. 24
Thomson Brandt 48, 66
Thomson-CSF 136
Tirole, J. 11, 47, 110
Titman, S. 19
TLC 98
Tobit regression 54
Togo 50
Tohamy, S. 34
Tokyo market, speculative bubble on the 36
Total Petroleum 29
Total-Fina Elf (formerly Elf
    Aquitaine) 98, 136
TPA *see* Third Party Access
Tractebel 108
trade-off between allocative and
    productive efficiency 10
trade union 52
trading
    in shares 14
        of privatized firms 71
    value of privatized companies 73-7
Transenser 109
transfer control 67
Trinidad and Tobago 29
    foreign investors in 29
Turkey 25, 128-9
    golden shares 138

ultimate ownership in privatized
    vs. matching private firms 87

unbundling 102
underpricing
  share offerings 78
  strategic 18, 60
unemployment 12–13, 28
unionization, levels of 28
United Kingdom (UK) 1, 5, 23–5, 41–2, 44,
      48–50, 70, 89, 94, 111, 120, 128, 139
  banks 24
  desegregated market structure 105
  golden shares 135–6
  Labour party 60
  Monopolies and Mergers Commission 89
  postal and transport services 51
  privatization process in 24, 51–2, 61
  rail infrastructure 66
  sale of utilities–water companies 24
  share issue privatizations (SIPs) 60
  under-pricing 60
United States (US) 30, 42, 44, 71, 90, 108,
      111, 128
  Exon-Florio Amendment (1988) 90
  exponential growth in capitalization and
      turnover 71
Uruguay 44, 128
  Banco Commercial 31
Usas Ucaç Servisi 138
US Enrichment Co. 28

Van Oijen, P. 71
van Randenborgh, M. 24
Veba 1
Venezuela 44, 110, 128
Verdier, T. 12–13, 15

VG 108
Vickers, J. 1, 5, 68, 99
Vickrey, W. 16
Vishny, R. W. 11, 28, 38, 40–1, 49–51, 79, 88
Volkswagen 1
VSNL 134

Wallsten, S. 111
walrasian market 40
Walsh, P. 6
Weber, R. 117
Weiss, L. 134
welfare economics, fundamental theorems of 6
Western Europe 21–3
  percentage of revenue for the sale of
      utilities 98–9
widely held firms 86
Wilfried Derksen's Electoral Web
      Sites 126–7
Wilhelm, W. J. Jr. 59–60
Williamson, O. 9, 101
Willig, R. D. 7, 10–11
Wint, A. G. 30
World Bank 1, 49–51, 69, 150
Wright, V. 25

Yarrow, G. 1, 5, 68, 99
Yergin, D. 5

Zarate's World Political Leaders
      since 1945 127
Zervos, S. 46, 69
Zhang, Y. 111
Zimbabwe 44, 128